# WEBINARS WITH

## WITH
# W<sub>O</sub>W
# FACTOR

by Becky Pike Pluth, M.Ed.
foreword by Bob Pike, CSP, CPAE

# DEDICATION

*To Raegan, Brody and Gabe*

Whose sweet "I love yous" keep me going even when I'm tired and ready to be done, and you are just getting started. Because of you, I have many tiny fingerprints on my computer screen and heart.

Thank you for "helping" mommy with her book and previewing pictures. Your votes count the most.

Thank you for coming into my office and sharing your sunny smiles a hundred times and asking if my book is done yet so I can come and play or pray.

This may not be the best bedtime reading, but your smiles make me feel like it is. You humble me.

# ENDORSEMENTS

*As our workforce is distributed, our learning and training must also go virtual. Becky's book provides the tools to design and deliver webinars the right way–interactive, creative, and engaging. Using these tools, you can match the learning that takes place in an instructor-led, participant-centered classroom.*

**ELLIOTT MASIE**
**CHAIR, THE LEARNING CONSORTIUM**

Webinars with Wow Factor *is clearly a valuable resource for anyone looking to use webinars as an effective tool. I have spread the word that this book is a "must read" for everyone in our organization involved in conducting webinars and look forward to improved results in our already successful webinar efforts because of this great book!*

**MIKE BRODERICK**
**CEO, TURNING TECHNOLOGIES, LLC.**

*If you've ever wondered how to create an effective online learning experience,* Webinars with Wow Factor *will be a great resource for you.*

**MAURICE HEIBLUM**
**PRESIDENT, ELLUMINATE, INC.**

*I thought your book was wonderful! I will definitely be using some of your tips and tricks in my work. There were so many times throughout reading that I thought, "Exactly!" or "Hmmm. Do I do that?" or "Oh, boy! We better start doing that!" Thank you for making me think deeper about what I do on a daily basis.*

**HEATHER CLEVENGER**
**WEBINAR AND PARTNER MARKETING MANAGER**
**ELLUMINATE, INC.**

*Webinars with WoW Factor:*
*Tips, Tricks and Interactive Activities for Virtual Training*
© copyright 2010 by Becky Pike Pluth, M.Ed. All rights reserved.

## Editorial Notation
For space considerations and ease of reading, the style guide for this book allowed for the use of "they," "them" and "their" following the use of an indefinite singular antecedent. This decision was made based upon the precedence set in classic literature and major dictionaries.

## Credits
Editor: Liz Wheeler
Book Designer/Illustrator: Jody Majeres, Majeres Graphic Design
Photography: Bigstock Photos

ISBN 13: 978-0-9794103-1-4
ISBN 10: 0-9794103-1-2

# CONTENTS

# ACKNOWLEDGEMENTS

Amidst the chaos of life, there is a serene oasis as I think about those who have helped me in this journey of writing my second book. To everyone who has interacted with me in a webinar over the past four years and has helped refine my process, perhaps without knowing it, I thank you.

As beautiful and gentle as the pitter patter of falling rain, I express my immense gratitude to family, friends and colleagues. Here is virtual applause.

To Bob Pike, my dad, for introducing me to interactive webinars and providing me the opportunity to spread my wings and soar through the elearning sky. After working with you for several years, I look forward to continuing it and would do it again. Thank you for sharing freely and helping me grow as a trainer.

To Liz Wheeler, for once again being the best "producer" I could ask for. You gave me space when needed but also encouraged me to pick up the pace, which helped me see the end. One of these days we won't have such a tight deadline and will be able to sleep before going to press! Thank you for using your gift with words to make this book flow.

To Sara Davis, for providing candid feedback when it was least convenient for you, helping me "see" my blind spots, and making this book more logical. Thank you for showing me you care in the ways I best receive it.

To Rob Pike, for your time and presence in helping motivate me to keep at it, even when there were so many other things to get done. Thank you for noticing the daily challenges and picking up the vacuum to clear the way for me to focus.

To Kendra Gruman, for making my webinars flow seamlessly. You were always up for the challenge, even when testing out new activities, which required a lot of backend help. It takes a team, and you have been the best. Thanks for patiently waiting for the return of the Killer Bunnies. I promise you, that day is near!

To Scott Enebo, Rich Meiss, Doug McCallum, Janice Horne, Priscilla Shumway, Adrianne Roggenbuck, Betsy Allen, Rich Ragan, Kathy Dempsey, Dave Arch, Bob Pike, Susan Gillen Kotok and Mary Jergens for saying yes to working with me and sitting through online sessions and activities for trainer meetings. Yes, you too are in this book as part of my study; perhaps some of the exercises look familiar! Thank you for having fun online and putting up with me as your producer.

To my faithful editors: Liz Wheeler, Dr. Sara K. Davis, Barb Pike and Sue Gillerlain. The book is readable! Thanks for turning around pages in hours and staying up late with me, again. Alas, there is calm after the storm, and, if you are reading this, the calm has arrived!

To Jody Majeres, you have once again illuminated my ideas. As for the cover, you nailed it! This is so me. I am passionate and enthusiastic about what I do with webinars, and you have graphically demonstrated that so well. Thank you, my dear friend.

To Barb Pike, my mom. Without you, this book wouldn't have been finished. You volunteered to watch my children when I had no nanny and a deadline looming. Thank you for reading over copy, like I was back in high school, challenging me to get an A.

To my best mate, who is proud of me on my worst days and astonished on my best days. You are my WoW Factor. Thank you for being my life mate and best friend. Until next time, cheers, Babe; this book is done!

To my Savior and Lord Jesus Christ, who has bestowed unto me undeserved grace and patience. You are the Rock in whom I put my trust. Thank you for rounding off my rough edges and loving me unconditionally. To God be the glory.

# FOREWORD

Webinars that WoW—is that title an oxymoron?

For most webinars it is.

For Becky Pike Pluth, and other trainers at The Bob Pike Group, it is not. Since the days of satellite broadcasts, we have designed distance and online learning to be interactive. From 10,000 people in 700 locations, to one person in one location, it can be done. You just need to know how. That's what this book does.

This book is not about theory, though it is instructionally sound. It is about delivering results—before, during and after a webinar. The first few chapters will give you a great foundation—one that has been field-tested with all the clients that have gone through The Bob Pike Group's "Webinars that Work" seminar, either live or online. The rest of the content is a series of customizable interactivities that allow you to instantly increase the impact of your webinars.

Everything that Becky recommends in her book has been field-tested over and over again, not only in our webinars but also in those we've helped our clients design and deliver. And, in all of that, Becky has been the champion. As vice president of training and development for The Bob Pike Group, she has been the driving force that has not only pulled together and documented all of the tools and techniques that we've developed over the years, but has used her own creative energies to add significantly to the body of work.

One specific example of her insight is the role of producer. For years, we have recommended having a moderator to help with the delivery of the webinar, as have many others. It was Becky who really brought into focus for our company the concept that the moderator is much more than that and is, in fact, the producer. People have resonated with that idea. It seems simple, but it is quite powerful and is a quantum leap in thinking. Implementing this change in role and perspective has added immeasurably to the impact of our webinars.

So get out a pen, some tape flags and a highlighter. Apply what you find in these pages, and you'll positively impact the results of your webinars.  You'll be well on your way to "Webinars with WoW!"

Bob Pike, CSP, CPAE, Speakers Hall of Fame
Chairman and CEO, The Bob Pike Group
Founder and Editor, *Creative Training Techniques* newsletter

# INTRODUCTION

Imagine yourself running around your office hooking up wires then turning on your computer and waiting impatiently for it to boot. As it's loading, you grab a huge three-ring binder, your heart racing. In two hours, you will be hosting your first webinar–with worldwide participants, no less.

During the webinar, you will have only three hours to get information into the hands of 30 vendors. At the end of the "call," they should be able to use the new system your company is rolling out.

The morning flies by. You have prepared as much as you can to use the webinar platform, but very little is written on how to host a virtual training well.

With your breathing labored, you begin your webinar and slowly ease into the role. Three hours later, you have lectured and read from hundreds of branded slides. Your managers praise your successful training and applaud the amazing job done. Unbeknownst to you or your managers, however, some of the participants on the other end of the "call" spent time emailing one another, conference calling, washing dogs, ordering groceries and renewing library books. Just because you've taught it, doesn't mean they've caught it.

I have learned that lecturing with PowerPoint® on the computer not only enables inertia, it can drive people to other distractions. So I began developing interactivities I could use to keep learners engaged during online training sessions.

This book is for anyone who has ever hosted an online webinar and wondered, "Is anyone out there actually listening?"

This book is a compilation of tools I have used to prepare for webinars and best practices for great synchronous training that engages the learner in a variety of ways to increase retention and keep facilitators from wondering, "Is anybody home?"

If you haven't hosted a webinar that is interactive, know that you can be effective just by applying a few of the tips, tricks and activities found in the following chapters. Start with the things that are easiest for you, and then, as you grow in confidence and ability, try out some of the intermediate or advanced techniques.

You can also save yourself a lot of time by purchasing the supplemental PowerPoint slides at WebinarsWithWowFactor.com. The PowerPoint decks of 60 pre-made slides for use in your own training are very affordably priced and will save you hours of design time.

If you have never done a webinar, check out a free one online and experience just how boring they can be, even if it is a topic you enjoy. Experience is a great teacher and having a foundation of what a webinar is will help bring to life what you read in this book.

To find a webinar, use your favorite search engine like Google, Bing or Dogpile and search the phrase "free webinar" to find sessions you can attend. Add a topic of interest to narrow the search.

# WHAT IS A WEBINAR?

A webinar is an online seminar that allows people from around the world to connect in a virtual classroom and share information via the internet. Webinars are a form of elearning because it uses a computer or mobile device as the classroom. I love Bill Horton's definition of elearning as "the use of information and computer technologies to create learning experiences."

Webinars are typically synchronous, meaning the instructor is on at the same time as the learner. One of the big benefits of webinars is the flexibility of attending the session from anywhere in the world without travelling. Some sessions utilize Voice over Internet Protocol (VoIP) which sends the instructor's voice over the internet digitally, and participants listen to the instructor through a headset plugged into their computer. Other webinars use a standard conference call connection where participants call into a conference bridge and talk over the phone.

When doing a webinar, companies need to select a platform, or virtual classroom program, to use. In appendix A, there is a list of different platforms for training. If you are just using the virtual classroom to host a meeting and not truly for training, there are a lot of other options. However, if you are using webinars to help learners retain information, the platform selection is critical in order to allow interaction to occur in a variety of ways, just as it is in the classroom.

The platform can make the difference between one classroom with only a whiteboard and another classroom with a variety of tools like music, flip charts, LCD projectors and more. The second classroom will allow for more interactivities and a variety of learning experiences. A company called WebEx has a platform for meetings called Meeting Center and one for training called, not surprisingly, Training Center. You can compare these two to get an idea of the differences between the platforms depending on their intended use.

# CHAPTER ONE

## WHERE DO I START?

Preparation to do a webinar starts with understanding what it is and how it should look, sound and feel. If you haven't already participated in at least one webinar, it would be to your advantage to do so before reading further. The differences between platforms and the different tools available will make a lot more sense if you have experienced them.

Assuming that a training slide deck used in a regular classroom can be put online and called a webinar is a huge mistake. In a classroom, there is automatic interaction and an ability to connect with others. The best webinars try to replicate that people connectivity as much as possible. Not all synchronous training is alike and getting a good feel for what is out there can help in the planning process.

Before designing your own, attend webinars on different platforms that are of varying lengths. This will allow you, as an instructional designer, to get the feel for different course lengths, what can be accomplished in a time frame, and how draining it can be on a learner. Taking notes on how distracted or engaged participants are can also help in preparing and designing.

Before a webinar even begins, there are elements of design that have to happen. In classroom training, it is called Instructional Design (ID) and, for elearning, it is called Instructional Systems Design (ISD). This book will cover, at a high level, some of the ISD elements needed for success, but there are numerous books on the topic that will bring you deeper. For a list of suggested books and resources, see appendix B.

The ADDIE model (Analysis, Design, Development, Implementation, Evaluation) is one of the most recognized forms of instructional design. Although it's only a five-step design process, there are hundreds of variations. The variation I recommend is done by the American Society for Training and Development.

At a glance, here is how the ADDIE model works. Each of the five steps feeds into the next step.

## *ANALYSIS PHASE*

In the analysis phase for webinars, just as it is for the classroom, the problem is clarified, goals and objectives are defined, and the learner's existing knowledge and skills are identified. Questions asked in this phase include:

- What is an organizational NEED?
- Who is the audience?
- Where is the audience located?
- What do they need to learn? Is there a gap or a future need?
- What is the behavioral outcome?
- What types of constraints exist?
- What other processes or systems will be impacted?
- What are the online pedagogical (teaching) considerations?
- What are the Adult Learning Theory considerations?
- What is the timeline for pilot, roll out and completion?

When given a client project, I find that doing a thorough analysis takes a lot of time and effort. Have you considered skipping the analysis phase? Likely the answer is yes. The problem with skipping the analysis phase for webinars is that there is no way to redirect or determine workarounds if you are totally missing the mark. Companies think this takes a lot of time, which it does, but how much more time and money is invested when programs are created and rolled out and then don't work? Perhaps the content was wrong or the audience didn't need the type of information shared.

At minimum, I recommend Bob Pike's concept of analysis using non-repetitive measures. Use a few different methods to find the information you need. Do surveys *and* observations or do interviews *and* focus groups. See if coming at the suggested problem in different ways results in the same solution. Find out if the problem is really the problem. The invested time will allow you to tailor the webinar to the need-to-know information.

Most people don't even know there are other methods to use for analysis beyond surveys, observations and focus groups. Try using on-the-job observations, ride-alongs, testing and assessments, task analysis or historical data gathering for variety. At a minimum, ensure there is a need for the training class and spend quality time designing and developing the class. Once online, there is little forgiveness for lack of planning and solid ISD.

## ASSESS AUDIENCE

There are always varying levels of knowledge with the subject matter being taught as well as varying levels of experience with the technology and webinar platform. When teaching a group that has little webinar experience, choose novice-level activities. This would include some whiteboard, poll and chat exercises. When doing needs analysis, it is important to ask who your audience is and how much experience they have in a synchronous classroom.

## WRITE OBJECTIVES

The designer needs to make sure that the analysis and design of the class is solid; the facilitator needs to audit the objectives, because he ultimately is responsible for how well the training solves the problem.

Those objectives should use verbs that are measurable. Verbs such as "understand," "know" and "learn" are not measurable. At the end of the webinar, how can it be assessed that one knows or understands? Objectives that can be measured will eliminate this problem.

# HERE IS A WELL-WRITTEN OBJECTIVE:

*By the end of the webinar, when given a list of 10 deadly sins of synchronous training, the learner will be able to verbally share how each can be avoided.*

This objective identifies the audience, the behavior, what conditions exist and to what degree the behavior will be mastered. Broken down it looks like this:

*Audience*–the learner
*Behavior*–share how each can be avoided
*Condition*–given a list of 10 deadly sins of synchronous training
*Degree of Mastery*–verbally

Objectives should be written for the learner and be evaluated during the session, not after. If it cannot be evaluated during the session, then there is no way to verify the lesson was grasped and mastered in the class to reproduce later. If someone is just learning to swim, wouldn't it be important to test and measure her ability during swim class before sending her into the ocean on her own? In the same way, your objectives should be written well before class and, like our swimmer's skill level, measured during class.

## DESIGN PHASE

The design phase is where you specify in detail what information you want to cover and put it in a logical order. During this phase, you might:
- Create detailed storyboards that define the instructional, visual and technical strategy,
- Determine content and instructional strategies, while keeping in mind the four domains (cognitive, affective, psychomotor, interpersonal),
- Design interactivities, which can include polling or assessments or choose some from this book (see the index for an easy-to-follow grid of activities), and
- Create prototypes to get an idea of how your interactions will look and feel. (You can create these in Microsoft® PowerPoint®, Apple® Keynote® or applications you will be

sharing from your computer such as Microsoft Outlook, AllPlay Web, BRAVO! or ResponseWare. See a list of resources in appendix C.)

## DEVELOPMENT PHASE

When we develop the training, we begin to move thoughts from paper and into the end product. Graphics are now created. Programmers might need to develop and integrate technologies. Test out any applications you plan to share via application sharing, and fix any errors. All documents you will need are created like handouts, a leader's guide, polling questions and feedback forms. If a pilot program is being run, it is done during this phase, and the feedback is then used to make adaptations and changes to the program.

Most professionals agree on the importance of ID. However in reviewing Brandon Hall's elearning directory, only 75 of more than 1,000 providers even talk about the link between their tool and ISD. Companies will talk a lot about how cool their tool is, but if they haven't a clue about solid ISD or how ISD links to their tool, be cautious. Test it out, see if it stands up to basic principles of adult learning theory, and assess if the tool will align with your design and evaluation needs.

## IMPLEMENTATION PHASE

Now that everything has been developed, it is "go" time. Everything is put into place during a training session. Each of the objectives should be met through the delivery of the content. During the implementation phase, a procedure for training the facilitators and the learners is developed. The facilitator should cover the course curriculum, learning outcomes, method of delivery and testing procedures.

This is also the phase where the producer (or others online assisting the facilitator) ensures that downloads, handouts and software are in place and that the learning application or website is functional. If things don't work, he is available to help troubleshoot and find solutions.

# EVALUATION PHASE

The final step has actually been happening all throughout the steps. Evaluation forms are designed and developed earlier in ADDIE, but here is where that information is compiled and analyzed to define how the session went and what needs improvement. This is a formative evaluation for the instructors and the design team. A summative evaluation can also be used to assess the participants' knowledge of the topic just covered. This is done through assessments given to the learners and then graded to identify gaps and ensure objectives were met.

While studying under Bob Pike, I learned the evaluation phase can be time consuming because revisions might change up to 50 percent of the original design. Expect changes, no matter how great the designer might be.

Ken Molay, president of Webinar Success, says actual attendance for free webinars for the general public is about 33 percent of those who registered. If you target a specialized audience, attendance goes up to about 50 percent. For internal training and employee communications, you might be lucky to get as high as 80 percent of those who registered, even if the event is mandatory.

Why such high default rates? Any number of things–from technical difficulties to brain numbing litanies–can contribute to this reluctance and truancy.

Synchronous training doesn't have to be this way, but few who experienced awful elearning are anxious to try it again to see how good elearning can be. If you have one shot at a great webinar, give it your all and start off right with strong design and interactivity built into it.

Turn to the ADDIE Model Overview in appendix B for a webinar grid for the ADDIE model. Along with examples of meetings that occur in each phase, you will find examples of tasks done in each phase of the design process. This high-level overview also suggests approximate time spent on each of the phases for a project.

# FOLLOW THE FOUR P'S

If time is short and you can't do ADDIE adequately, use the four P's as an easy checklist to quickly gauge your readiness: Plan, Prepare, Practice, Perform. In appendix D, you can find a list of tasks to think about in each phase of the webinar. Use this list in conjunction with the four P's.

## PLAN

### ANALYZE

Assuming that some type of needs assessment has been done by your client, look through that information and identify who the learners are and what their knowledge, skills and abilities are. What depth of knowledge do they need to have at the end of the class? Take the time now to write objectives for the learner, the manager and the business. Each has its own unique interest in the session, and all needs should be satisfied.

### KNOW THE CONTENT

When I'm facilitating, I don't need to be an expert on the content– I just need to know a little bit more than those I'm teaching. If you are teaching a topic that may have a lot of specialty questions, such as the roll out of a new software or system, invite a subject matter expert (SME) to participate in the webinar as a guest speaker to answer any detailed questions and build question-and-answer times into the webinar. Prepare the SME in advance, and use a timer that all can see to help stick to the timing allotted for the session.

### PROJECT SCOPE

In the appendices, you'll find one titled Tasks Required to Design, Produce and Deliver a Participant-centered Webinar Checklist (appendix E). The checklist has every step listed in a fairly chronological order so that nothing gets missed. Each platform has its own unique features, so there may be a few additional aspects to think about on a case-by-case basis. Another aspect that will modify this checklist is if the session is being hosted for hundreds of people at one time with multiple trainers managing multiple virtual classrooms. Oftentimes, there are restrictions to platform usability in these instances, and these sessions tend to be far more rigid and more like meetings than trainings.

How many people should be in a class? For training purposes, I recommend 25 learners to one producer and one facilitator. Each additional participant makes it more difficult to manage the class, engage all learners, use the tools and have learners feel connected.

## WEBINAR TEAM MEMBERS

There are three main roles in every training webinar. The first is that of the facilitator or trainer. Because I train in the classroom as well as online, I go by the latter. Whatever you choose to call yourself, be consistent. The trainer is responsible for much of the design and development and, once the session begins, is accountable for the delivery of the content.

Training online is very different from in the classroom. A rock star classroom trainer or keynoter does not automatically make a good online presenter. When teaching in a webinar, there are no smiling faces, no audible laughter and no opportunity to ensure a learner is sitting at the computer and absorbing information. You cannot rely on watching the room to know when an engaging exercise needs to be done. It has to be pre-planned and executed with enthusiasm.

Creating an engaging learning environment online is more than just having learners text chat one another constantly, or having them read from slides. It is about keeping them involved in a variety of ways– building a community where they get to know one another so they don't feel isolated. This can be done by welcoming participants as they enter the "room" and scrolling questions to be answered as others are still logging in.

When I was producing for a colleague, he greeted the participants and asked them questions, and they turned on their microphones to respond. I could hear interest by both sides and feel the camaraderie, although I could not see it. The relationships built prior to the session, continued all throughout the session, and learners found themselves not wanting to miss a moment. When you feel responsible to someone else in the room and are held accountable to everyone through participation in polls, breakout rooms, material reviews and teach-backs, it is far more difficult to get distracted by all the other things online and in the office.

As the trainer is guiding participants down the learning trail, the producer works to circumnavigate any road blocks or delays and is ready with a backup plan should technology fail.

The producer should have administrative rights to the session so she can fulfill her platform-task responsibilities like creating and sending participants into breakout rooms, clearing whiteboards, putting up correct polling buttons, and answering text chat questions as they come in. The producer manages pretty much anything in the background so the trainer's focus can be on the content and not on the logistics.

The producer can also step in as a participant if another person is needed for partners or role-plays.

The final role is that of the learner. Help create an environment that is safe and enjoyable for learners by having them come prepared. Send them a welcome letter with instructions on how to successfully log in and state specifically what the computer requirements are. When details are covered and a novice participant successfully logs in for the first time, there is a lot of motivation, positive energy and can-do attitude a trainer can draw from. Poor planning, on the other hand, can set you so far back, you may never be able to get learners motivated again.

As you plan, put yourself in the learners' shoes and take a look at their view. Always look for times to thank them for participating and sharing, reward their involvement, and encourage them to look for ways to adapt, adopt and apply the content back on the job. Encouragement goes a long way for participants on the other side of the monitor.

# PREPARE

## FOLLOW THE 90/20/4 RULE

No matter the length of a webinar, there should always be interactivity. Training expert Bob Pike says adults can listen with understanding for 90 minutes before they need some sort of mental and physical break. He also says there should be reflection time every 20 minutes. He uses the example of an empty water glass to represent the learners' capacity to absorb 20 minutes of information. Water is the content. "As information is poured into the glass, it begins to overflow after 20 minutes," Pike says. "With water being made up of particles, there is no way to know which particle, or piece of information in this case, is being retained. By giving learners time to apply the learning to real life or practice tasks, retention is increased."

Based on my experiences with webinars and research I've done, the average length of time a learner stays engaged before getting distracted and begins a new task is 4 minutes. This means that, unless I want to lose my learners to email, and online bill paying, I need to engage participants every 4 minutes.

Interaction comes in various forms. Learners might read, write in a workbook, type on the whiteboard, reflect, listen to different voices, poll or chat.

The more inexperienced the webinar audience is with the platform and the content, the more focused they are on trying to stay with the facilitator. Their distractions are typically user error and time spent with a producer trying to figure out where they are and what they are supposed to be doing.

The more advanced the user is with either the subject matter or the webinar tools, the quicker they get distracted and the more likely they are to leave their computer and run to the grocery store or do laundry! These true stories happen because facilitators are designing synchronous training as though it were a conference call.

If participants know they are not going to be "watched" or expected to do more than listen, then they can get away with being distracted. As a solution, have designers plan for interaction from the very moment the virtual classroom opens and every 4 minutes thereafter. Use the Design Templates in appendix F to make sure there is something engaging your learners regularly.

## CREATE ACTIVE LEARNING ACTIVITIES

When opening a building toy like LEGOS bricks, there is usually an image of something that can be built, along with the instructions. What makes LEGOS bricks fun? Their flexibility–a choice of either reading the instructions or ignoring them and diving right in to create something. There is not a right or a wrong. If there are parts left over, it just leaves more for creating another object.

But what if there was only one item that could be made and each time it was done, it was created in the exact same order, piece by piece? How many times would someone enjoy the process? After the third or fourth time, it gets old. The same is true when learning. If the same activities are repeated with little or no variation, the learner once again begins to tune out the lesson and goes back to emailing or harvesting crops on their virtual farm.

Active learning involves the learner and compels them to read, speak, listen, think deeply, write (fill-in-the-blanks and separate notes pages on the whiteboard or chat area), brainstorm, problem-solve or even laugh.

Active learning activities go back to the teachings of Socrates. It puts learners in a position where they are the ones doing the work. They are experiencing the technology, the problem, the product. Active learning requires thinking.

A well-crafted lecture only requires low-level comprehension where a listener may write down notes, but he is left unchanged. Change is what makes an interactive webinar different. Retention is increased, and that is done through the participation of every learner on a regular basis throughout the session. So many webinars don't integrate this, which is why webinars often are attended by login only.

If active learning is employed, attendance will go up as well as retention, because attendees are involved and doing. This book provides you with ideas to get learners engaged, excited and interested in the content being taught. By inserting your content into the activity frames, you will save yourself a lot of time!

Another great companion resource is the PowerPoint decks for these activities. These slides will save you hours of searching for just the right slide,  save you the cost of purchasing the rights for use, and will spare you the tedium of attempting to create engaging slides. The companion decks are available at WebinarsWithWowFactor.com and follow the PowerPoint design principles covered in chapter 3.

## SELECT CHAMPIONS OR CAPTAINS

When teaching in any setting, think about having champions of the training session. For a webinar training, these champions are the "go-to" people after the class. If it is a technical session, they may have been the pilot participants who typically have a bit more content depth, so they are able to provide support or solutions to others. If the webinar is reaching out to nine branches, there would be a champion or captain at each branch.

Champions should have a supportive attitude about the topic. In general, they are peers to the learners. This is important because learners work harder for each other. These individuals should have a positive spirit and be encouraging as well as willing to give candid feedback to the designers so that enhancements can be made. Use champions to help promote the upcoming webinars and market the training, as well as on the backend for follow-up on training issues or bridging content. Here are a few Dos and Don'ts for learning captains or champions to think about:

## LEARNING CHAMPION DOS AND DON'TS

| DO | DON'T |
|---|---|
| Talk about the webinar training with staff: what it will do for the company, what impact it will have, next steps for learning. | Feel like you have to be a subject matter expert. Just know where to go to find the answers. |
| Focus your attention on a few influential team members. Meet one-on-one to help motivate them and encourage their support of the training. Ask for their support. | Guess at the answers. |
| Find co-champions. They can be just as effective at speeding up the change or learning process. Support them and reward them with encouragement and praise. | Hesitate to ask for advice or help. |
| Involve all and make them aware of what the champion is there for. | Be a one-person show. Collaborate with other champions to see what they are doing. |
| Wear a shirt following the training that makes it easy for them to see who to ask for help. It may mean wearing the same shirt for three days. | Forget food and treats. These make feedback sessions far more enjoyable. |
| Invite others to give feedback and ask questions about the training. Provide support and alleviate concerns by troubleshooting and directing them to the answers. | Be intimidated by how much work being a champion can be. A champion might invest 30-60 minutes a day focusing on this aspect of the job. |
| Host feedback sessions. Share learnings and how the new knowledge is being used. Make topics fun: "Secret Shortcut Keys Identified." | Skip getting feedback from those implementing the webinar content. |
| Recognize staff who embrace the learning. Be sincere. | Keep learnings to yourself. Share with other champions, trainers and management. |
| Publicize results. | Forget or hide results because it didn't go perfectly. |

## ON-LINE EVALUATION

Every webinar should have an evaluation. No matter the length of the training, a simple three-question survey or poll will get participants to share their immediate reactions to the session. When creating an evaluation, think about the types of questions you want to ask and how the data will be used after the session.

There is a science to surveys and people have doctorates in Survey and Usability. There are entire books on the topic if you should want to learn more. Here are a few of the most common types of questions and the type of scale that should be used for each.

If I am doing a four-part webinar, I use a three-question evaluation for the first three days. On the final day, I use the same three-question evaluation for that day, and then I give a full evaluation for feedback on the course overall. This provides me with day-by-day insight versus only an overall view. I can then make changes to the right sections instead of guessing.

I use a five-point scale, and the three questions I ask are:

- *How useful was the content?*
- *How present were you?*
- *How effective was the instructor?*

Appendix G includes typical evaluation questions along with the type of scale used. When using different scales, make sure the scale is posted on the screen and only questions with the same scale are on the slide. Use a different slide for different scales.

# PRACTICE

## BE FAMILIAR WITH THE SOFTWARE

One of the most common reasons webinars do not go well is because of user error with software. When hosting a webinar, practice the online tools, and be familiar with any and all tools that will be used. Tools could include those within the webinar platform, those applications that might be shared, and conference-calling technology. Familiarity with these also increases facilitator confidence and reduces anxiety.

## PREPARE TO TEACH IN THE ONLINE MEDIUM

Preparing includes practicing everything from logging in and uploading the slides to walking through each slide and tool to be used. For example, if an application is going to be shared from one desktop to another, it is imperative the facilitator and producer know how to manage the tools to do this seamlessly. It also helps the producer and facilitator understand how their roles will work together.

If you are co-facilitating, then do a walk-through of how transitions will happen. When first co-facilitating an online session, novices will often say exactly what is going to happen: "I am now going to hand off the session to Steve who will talk about the next slide." Instead, work together to have easy transitions between facilitators. Do this by having one facilitator set-up and lead an activity and the other debrief the activity that feeds into the next content piece. See appendix H: Checklist for Co-facilitation.

## EXPERIENCE IT AS A LEARNER

It is important to not only be able to technically share the application but also to experience the application sharing as a learner. In some platforms when application sharing, the learner's desktop doesn't show the whole application unless the user enlarges the window with the application. Unless the facilitator has experienced the tool as a learner, this little fact may get passed by and the participants may get lost in the sharing and not say anything. When these little things are discovered, keep a log of what to say to participants so they can be successful.

## HAVE A BACKUP PLAN

What will you do when the system fails or the conference bridge goes out? When working with technology, it is very common that something will happen during a synchronous training. Having a backup plan allows for flexibility and usually pays off.

If the platform boots learners off, having a plan as simple as saying, "Let's take an 'een' break! Time for caffeine, nicotine, latrine, magazine or answering machine. Thirteen-minute break and meet back in the virtual classroom. This gives you enough time to do a couple of things but doesn't give you enough time to do all! You choose. See you in thirteen!" I got this from a participant years ago and have been using it faithfully ever since.

## PERFORM

When it is go time, be dynamic. Co-hosts that are diverse "characters" add interest (men, women; voices that are different; perspectives that are unique). It also provides an opportunity to role model the qualities of collaboration you want to instill in others.

If you have prepared well, your PowerPoint will be a great slideshow, used as a visual backdrop. This sets the stage for a great, engaging session. Learners will know right away that you won't be reading to them and will appreciate it.

Keeping your 4-minute timed agenda is helpful, but have it flow naturally. You can use a roadmap for your learners with key content pieces but no timing listed so they know what's ahead.

Keep an uncluttered workstation so that it is easy to find reference material and the session flows you've worked out. Use the leader's guide, and keep track of timing as the session goes along. It is okay to end early. If it is a course for credit, have additional content in the learner's handbook that can be covered versus trying to stretch the content. When the pace is slow, distracters abound.

Make sure that the planned breaks happen between the 60- to 90-minute time frame. Learners need a chance to rest their tired computer eyes, stretch and use the restroom. You will thank yourself when both you and the participants come back invigorated and ready to absorb more information.

Before ending, help everyone see how much they accomplished together by having the learners summarize their top takeaways and key facts. Ending with time for learners to reflect on the content and add key learnings to a notes page allows each participant to find the "what's in it for me" element.

# CHAPTER TWO

## THE DEADLY SINS OF WEBINARS

Think about your last frustrating webinar experience. What was the problem? Why wasn't it a 10 on the scale of greatness? Chances are at least one of the deadly sins of webinars was committed. Part of avoiding sins is knowing what they are and what to do if unforeseen challenges come up. There are four people that can commit sins and, as the facilitator, you are the one responsible for preventing them!

## DEADLY SINS COMMITTED BY FACILITATORS

The facilitator is responsible for the entire learning community: how content is shared, timing and pacing, interactions of the learners, going through the ADDIE model, and so on. Here are just a few of the deadly sins that the facilitator is able to control and prevent if she takes the time to do so in the planning stage. This list also describes a lot of the roles and responsibilities of the trainer/facilitator.

### NOT STARTING OR ENDING ON TIME

Log in early and reward those ready to go by starting on time. If you regularly start late, learners that are ready will learn there's no point in being punctual. I use the first few minutes to review briefly how to use the tools for the day. If learners miss that, they will be frustrated because they don't know how to participate fully; have the producer watch who isn't in the room and have him work with those people on an individual basis. Let learners know in advance that the first few minutes will lay the groundwork for a successful session. If they can't make it on time, send a playback link to a previously recorded mini-session that goes through how to use the platform tools.

## NOT HAVING A SOFT OPENER

A few slides to begin engaging the learners before the session helps to warm up the brain similar to warming up before a run. Soft openers could be puzzles, word pictures, visual images or word searches. Skip the scrolling slides that only welcome participants and begin creating a learning community. Use a soft opener to break preoccupation and get participants thinking about the content.

## NOT HAVING A HANDOUT

Even if the handout is only an empty page that allows for interaction with the content, it is a start and much better than having no direction for learners. Most people want to know, even at a high level, what is going to be covered and what the key elements are. I have a hard time listening to keynote speeches that do not have a handout. Oftentimes, I am left feeling like we jumped all over, and I'm not sure what I'm supposed to take away. Was there a point? Or was I just supposed to be entertained or motivated?

Handouts create clarity and incorporate at least three principles of how people remember:
- handouts are visual,
- it is easier to recall information when learners have recorded it, and
- sections are chunked so it's easier to absorb and assimilate information.

## NO BACKUP PLAN

Ten people are ready to log in and the link doesn't work; now what? It's always best to plan for the worst and hope for the best. On the next page are some possible problems and best practice solutions.

| POSSIBLE PROBLEMS | BEST PRACTICE SOLUTIONS |
|---|---|
| Lack of technology | Pre-work, send materials |
| Loss of audio | Wait, have back-up conference call line |
| VoIP lag time for some learners | Have a teleconference bridge ready |
| Lack of participation | Use small groups, keep things moving, use polling features to assess pace, use team leaders |
| Technical difficulties | Have support person online, have a producer to troubleshoot with individuals so you can stay focused |
| Materials don't arrive | Create PDFs prior to mailing and email to participants |
| Confusing or abstract topic | Do pre-planning and have some pre-work for learners to gain familiarity with topic |
| Lag time | Allow for it … be willing to pause, have independent work available for learners to work on |
| Do not understand the materials | Ask questions to ensure comprehension, have other facilitators and learners preview materials and give feedback to prevent |
| Network goes down | Take a 15-minute break, even if a break just occurred; have everyone log back in at a specified time, pre-plan a date/time for a make-up session |
| Phones go down | Text chat to everyone and take a 15-minute break so IT can work on solution |
| Handouts won't download | Have a PDF version and email |
| Slower learners | Use a producer to assist those people |
| People unable to login | Have the tech support number available, verify the link and resend to group, create a new room and move into that session |

*Figure 2.1*

## NOT ENOUGH INTERACTION

Plan some interaction every 4 minutes. If I plan a poll and it takes 2 minutes to complete, then I need to have another engagement 4 minutes from the finish time of that poll. A schedule might look like this:

| TOTAL TIME | TIMING OF INTERACTIONS (EVERY 4 MINUTES) | TOPIC/ CONTENT | TYPE OF INTERACTION | MATERIALS/ PPT |
|---|---|---|---|---|
| 7:55-8:00 | 7:55-8:00 | Soft Opener | Word search | Hyperlink |
| 8:00-8:05 | 8:03 | Opener | Map locator | |
| 8:05-8:10 | 8:07, 8:10 | Agenda/ Objectives | Fill-in-the-blanks | Agenda slide |
| 8:10-8:25 | 8:14-8:18, 8:22 | Content | Whiteboard, brainstorming | |
| 8:25-8:35 | 8:26-8:31, 8:35 | Content | Read article/ highlight workbooks | |
| 8:35-8:45 | 8:39, 8:43 | Content | Polling | A-E multiple choice |
| 8:45-8:50 | 8:47 | Content | Text chat | Quick question/ response |
| 8:50-8:52 | 8:50 | Evaluation | Polling | Pre-made questions |
| 8:52-8:55 | 8:52-8:55 | Application | Handout, reflection | Workbook |
| 8:55-9:00 | 8:57 | Closer | Whiteboard, annotate | "Top Takeaways" page |

*Figure 2.2*

## TOO MUCH CONTENT

Webinars are for "need-to-know" information only. If learners won't be using the information multiple times in the next 30 days, the chances are slim that it will be retained when it is finally needed. Instead, teach learners how to search for the nice-to-know information and practice that multiple times so when the time comes and the information is needed, they can search for it. Challenge subject matter experts on what is truly need-to-know information. It takes about 33 percent more time to train online interactively compared to the classroom, which squeezes out the nice-to-know information.

## POOR PACING

Many facilitators and trainers are focused on flow, timing and a lot of other details, and it is easy to forget to check-in with learners to find out if they are comfortable with the level of detail and ready to move on. Teach learners at the beginning how to use their pacing tools and give them permission to ask for the session to be sped up or slowed down. Pause the session occasionally to ask how the pace is for the learners. This will give you a pulse and give learners a chance to feel comfortable giving feedback. If a majority of the group wants to slow down, slow down. If only one person is regularly asking for a quicker pace, consider giving them additional tasks like being a team scribe or time keeper. This will help keep them engaged while others take notes or problem solve.

## TOO MANY PEOPLE TALKING AT ONCE

When using VoIP, there can be a lot of feedback when multiple users all have their microphones on. This can be distracting. Practice calling on participants and having them raise their hands electronically to share; it will reduce the double voices and feedback for all. Have learners turn on their microphones when talking and back off when they are finished. The producer can also help by turning off mics that were left on accidentally.

## TOO MUCH TEXT ON SCREEN

PowerPoint puke is in the past. No more 700-word slides that are read. Slides should aid the presenter, not be the presenter. This rule applies to pre-made slides, not the slides participants create themselves. Instead of text, use images and photographs to depict ideas and concepts. In the next chapter, there are a lot of examples and ideas on making your PowerPoint interactive and usable.

## USING TOO MANY TOOLS

Just because a trainer knows how to use the tools doesn't mean all of them need to be used. It reminds me of a participant that went through The Bob Pike Group's Train-the-Trainer Boot Camp class. She went back to work so excited she decided to test everything out and amazingly implemented more than 30 ideas in a 30-minute meeting. Her company culture was used to lectures, and the interactive culture shock was over the top. Implementing one or two ideas would have been better. As learners got used to those engagement techniques, she could have added a few more or tried something different. Pretty soon the group buys into the interaction because the change is gradual.

Online is the same way. Just because a trainer knows the platform doesn't mean the learners do. Overuse tools and the session becomes a juggling act. Juggling one ball or two balls is manageable for all, but, as more balls are added, it becomes more difficult and nearly impossible for those of us who haven't learned the skill. More time is spent trying to get participants up to speed on where to find tools than it is on the actual content itself.

## NOT PRACTICING

Winging it won't work. If someone hasn't practiced the webinar, it typically becomes an online lecture. To avoid this, plan what tools you want to use during each of the activities and energizers. Give thought to the steps and practice pulling up each of the tools and giving clear directions. Give thought to how many participants will text chat or whiteboard at a time and what to do if they write on top of one another. Take the time to be confident with the tools. It provides more flexibility for the session and also makes the webinar more seamless.

## LECTURE, LECTURE, LECTURE

Death by lecture (also the title of a good book by Sharon Bowman) is one way to kill motivation. Instead, build in interactive learning activities from this book. Test out one interaction and see how things go. If you aren't enthusiastic about the activities, the participants won't be either, so begin with the exercises that are easiest and more your style. "I have to lecture," some might say. I am a recovering lecturer as well, and here you can start down the road to recovery. Admitting it is the first step.

Here are a few ideas to get you started:
- Break up lectures into smaller 4-minute lecturettes,
- Have participants be guest presenters on content they have expertise in,
- Use a short video clip to teach a section,

- Allow for learners to digest information by jotting down action ideas in their workbooks,
- Ask questions throughout the lecture and have learners text chat; use their examples and ideas.

## APPEARING (OR BEING) DISORGANIZED

If learners think the facilitator is clueless or disorganized, credibility is lost and hard to regain. Be consistent in where you place items you will use. If demonstrating the use of props on the webcam, have them readily available on the desk. If sharing a link to a website, check the link the morning of the session and have it ready to paste in. When application sharing your desktop, be sure to clear or file miscellaneous documents and shortcuts not needed for the session. The appearance of organization goes a long way, and it does help in maintaining an organized session and platform.

## IMPROPER HANDLING OF QUESTIONS

The purpose of a question in an online webinar is for learning to take place, not testing. Most sessions I have attended either run out of time or spend too much time on one question. If the answer goes beyond the 4 minutes, I'm not listening; I'm queuing my movies on NetFlix.

Allow participants time to process or craft questions in sub groups. This increases the buy-in for all and eliminates questions that are not valid or can be answered by another learner. Allow learners to "ask three before you ask me" when it comes to content that has already been covered. This encourages other learners to adapt and assimilate the information enough to help bring another up to speed.

## NO EVALUATION

Smiley sheets and feedback forms are used in the classroom on a regular basis but when it comes to online training, they are nowhere to be found. In webinars where I've been an attendee, more than 65 percent of the facilitators didn't have any type of evaluation at any point during their session. How do they know if I was bored and not participating? How will they know if several concepts were over my head?

They won't. They may feel like they did a great job because 50 people logged in, but when I log out at the end of the session, there may be only 11 left in the room. After only a few minutes, participants not paying for a webinar will log out if it isn't worth their investment of time. Keep them engaged and ask for feedback to make the next session even better.

# DEADLY SINS COMMITTED BY PRODUCERS

The producer is the person who takes care of many technical and logistical responsibilities before, during and after a webinar.  This person offers invaluable assistance to the trainer and makes sure that everything gets taken care of behind the scenes so that the trainer can focus on the material and the participants. During the course of the webinar, there are several things that the producer should pay attention to and simply take care of as they happen. When it doesn't happen, then it becomes a deadly sin. This list describes a lot of the roles and responsibilities of the producer.

### NOT SHOWING UP

Having the producer be a no-show has happened, and when a trainer is expecting support but doesn't receive it, he starts off baffled and needs to overcome angst and a raw set of nerves while trying to juggle an even larger number of tasks. A producer must be reliable and on time or early. Not showing up for the session until it is almost over can be disastrous to the class, especially if there are several tasks to be done.

### NOT OPENING THE TELECONFERENCE

Not only should the teleconference line be opened well in advance of learners logging on, but the producer should also know how to turn it on quickly should VoIP go out. Having a learner request it because of bandwidth issues and not being able to successfully connect them is deadly for all. Plan ahead for practicing this amidst a session and in the moment. If you haven't had to do this in awhile, a quick refresher is a good idea.

## NOT TESTING MEDIA AHEAD OF TIME

It is the producer's responsibility to log in early and make sure slides are loaded and working properly as well as any other media that may be used for the session. Planning ahead and doing a little bit of technical troubleshooting saves a lot of time and headaches later.

## NOT KNOWING THE PLATFORM

The producer is a technical resource and should know the platform and technology well enough that she can answer basic questions and do minor troubleshooting for the different tools. Each platform has its own user guide; the producer should have a copy of this and be ready to provide answers quickly. When a producer isn't able to quickly put up a timer or get people swiftly into breakout rooms, technology begins to take center stage instead of the content. She should also be able to assign tool permissions and set up breakout rooms in advance. It also means having Information Technology (IT) and the support number for the platform on speed dial.

## FORGETTING TO RECORD

When a session needs to be recorded for future replay, and the producer forgets to engage the recorder, this could be a problem for everyone. I recommend starting the recording before the session starts and letting it go for the entire length of the session. You can edit out any unnecessary breaks later.

I once paused a recording for a break in an effort to save on editing time; however, I forgot to start it again and this "shortcut" ended up backfiring. Lesson learned. Planning to edit is better than not having anything to edit at all.

## NOT ANSWERING TEXT CHAT QUESTIONS

Participants need attention when they have questions. If the question was posted to the group, but scrolls off the screen before the trainer has a chance to respond, the producer should privately text chat the trainer the identical question. If a learner privately text chats the producer, the producer should respond to that question in kind.

Text questions are like being on hold; check back in from time to time and give a status update so learners don't think you have forgotten them. Once when I was producing, a question was posed to me. I did not know the answer, so I began to search quickly for a response. In the meantime, the person texted me again; I hadn't bothered to let him know what I was doing the first time. So this time, I did respond with what I was doing and told him I would get back to him in just a minute or two.

## UNRESPONSIVE OR PASSIVE TOWARD PARTICIPANT AND INSTRUCTOR NEEDS

If participants do not come back from break or lunch, give them a call or send an email to make sure that everything is okay. When a producer doesn't respond to learner needs, it reflects directly on the trainer and the class as a whole. In the evaluation, there should be one or two questions related to the producer and his ability as well as his attitude toward helping participants.

## LACKING INITIATIVE

If a producer needs to be micromanaged and get specific, detailed directions for everything, it adds another level of stress for the facilitator. A producer should be self-directed and reliable. When there is something that needs to be taken care of, the producers is the go-to person. If the trainer's sound fails and he needs to leave the room and log back in, the producer should be ready to jump in and get learners into an activity so that it isn't a big deal and time is not wasted on waiting.

## NOT STAYING FOCUSED

Some might believe producing is a cushy job because there is so much free time in-between producer tasks. MISTAKE! A producer should be keeping track of timing, saving screenshots for future reference, adding to notations on the whiteboard, saving whiteboard slides, helping learners with their tools for whiteboarding, or setting up polling among other tasks the trainer has requested.

When a producer gets side tracked, she begins to miss cues for breakout rooms, not paste notes on the whiteboard or in the text chat area, have late or absent application launches, and neglect answering questions. Playing video games and ordering swimsuits are not part of the producer's task list. She needs to put away the PDA and take good notes to share with the facilitator after the session.

# DEADLY SINS COMMITTED BY MANAGERS

Managers play a big role in whether learning occurs or not. If a manager chooses not to let an employee participate in the webinar, then nothing can be learned or transferred back to the job. The manager's role in a webinar is to provide a safe environment for their employees to take the class, support the process, and help minimize distractions surrounding the employees while the webinar is going. It also means providing the support for systems and firewalls to be working so they can be successful. However, there are several things a manger can do to destroy the learning process for a webinar participant. Here are a few of a manager's deadly sins:

### PUTTING DOWN THE CLASS

Sharing negative opinions about the content or the trainer and making the employee feel dumb for even attending can kill any positive job-based outcome from the webinar. The session hasn't even begun and already the employee doesn't want to be there. This makes the trainer's job more difficult because now there are additional barriers, beyond technology, to overcome.

### INTERRUPTING

Receiving 10 emails in the first half hour all marked high priority removes the participant from the classroom. It's like knocking on the door of the training room 10 times and asking to speak to the same employee. Just because the class is online and the learner has access to email doesn't mean he is available to answer or respond. An interactive class keeps a learner working and learning all throughout with little time to respond to vague emergencies.

27

## NOT FOLLOWING UP

After the session, managers seem to rarely follow up to discuss an on-going action plan or ideas on how to implement the learning. This is a mistake because it doesn't encourage the learner to action plan. In fact, it promotes passive participation because there isn't accountability for having learned anything anyway.

## HOVERING

Being a helicopter manager doesn't make learning the content easier. Walking by the employee's office too many times makes him conscious he is being watched, which increases his tension, decreases retention, and reduces his participation on the webinar. Stay away and give them space to breath, kick back and enjoy the process of learning online. Don't ask why he is shooting baskets into imaginary trash cans; just know it is all part of the learning process.

## HAVING MULTIPLE PARTICIPANTS SHARE

Saving a few bucks and having a group interact as one person can take away from their online experience. Having one person "drive" while the others sit back isn't fun and doesn't enhance learning; allow learners to be individuals and take the class for themselves. Let them draw on their own whiteboards and talk in their own breakout rooms. The ability to learn the material is largely connected to those interactions and application.

# DEADLY SINS COMMITTED BY LEARNERS

Learners are responsible for their own engagement, focus, ability to learn and self-motivation. They walk in with prior knowledge, skills and abilities that can help the classroom to thrive and become a catalyst for learning. Participants should come prepared to learn and discover with open minds. Here are some of the biggest sins I have encountered.

## JOHNNY COME LATELY

Technology takes time to boot up and log into not to mention the added delays of server speeds and streaming. If a trainer has decided to stream a video and a song or two, that will slow learners' log in.

Encourage them to log in at least 15 minutes before and get the audio set-up done before going to get another cup of caffeine. Logging in late is even worse because now they have missed all the tool practice and are lost or are using up valuable producer time to get up to speed.

## THE SOCIALIZER

Sending private text and being sarcastic or inappropriate is a webinar no-no. This can be prevented by setting ground rules as a group and setting expectations ahead of time. Most people want to do the right thing, but that is hard to do if they don't have clear rules to guide them. Peers will hold one another accountable so the trainer and producer don't have to. Be sure to switch up breakout rooms so that the socializers don't exhaust their peers.

## THE DISENGAGED OR UNRESPONSIVE

When attending a class that is participant-centered, the one individual that doesn't poll, add a thought, raise a hand or share can be a nightmare. This person needs to be connected with one-on-one by the producer. Ask a question like, "It appears your tool bar isn't working; is there something I can help you with?" Once they know you have noticed them, it is surprising how they come to life.

Another trick is to choose team leaders to help with tasks. You can choose team leaders by telling them it is the person who raises a hand last or not at all!

## THE COMPLAINER

When participants consistently find things wrong with your webinar– the music you play, the tools being used, the questions asked–they are doing at least four things: focusing on the wrong thing, creating a distraction for the facilitator and producer, and eating up valuable con- necting time while sucking the life out of you. They may also be tak- ing away from their peers' ability to learn, depending on how they are sharing the feedback. When this sin arises, gently ask them to refrain from sharing feedback, but let them know there will be an opportunity for feedback at the end.

## THE DISTRACTED

The learner that logs in and then walks away from the computer to run errands, take a shower, yell at kids or bathe their dog is distracted. Clients have come to The Bob Pike Group asking me what they can do to get these things to stop. One client shared that a participant got her kids ready, yelled at them to hurry up, swore as the milk spilled on the floor and so on for 35 minutes. There were 200 people on the webinar, and there was no way to mute her phone on the conference call. If a participant-centered class has engagement every 4 minutes, these distractions become less frequent.

## DODGE THESE DISTRACTIONS

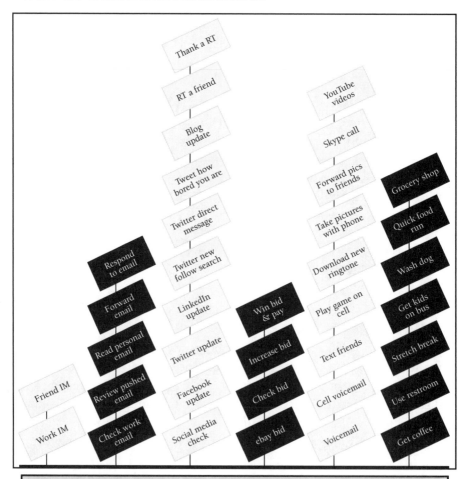

WORK-RELATED TRAINING WEBINAR – LOGGED IN

# CHAPTER THREE

## POWERPOINT, POLLING AND PARTICIPANT HANDOUTS

One of the basic ways to create graphic displays for webinars is through the use of PowerPoint or Keynote. However, taking a slide designed for an in-person meeting or training doesn't always work online. In a classroom, content often creeps into the "nice-to-knows," but information in a webinar should be strictly need-to-know. Reading through slides is not "good synchronous training."

In *Presentation Zen*, Garr Reynolds, a self-termed "design evangelist" and management professor, says people can't listen and read at the same time and, unless you are reading the slide verbatim, your learners are only focusing on listening or reading—not both. If the words match the message exactly, then why not just send the slides and forget the training? Instead, the slide should be an image or picture that represents the message being shared. Whiteboard slides (often created in PowerPoint and uploaded as a presentation) should be interactive and allow for discussion.

---

•Too many words for a simple activity

### Stretch Break

POORLY DESIGNED

Timing should be clear and not spelled out-use numbers

**Activity**
•Take a half minute and stretch. The body gets very tired when stagnant, so it is important for us to get the blood flowing.
•When stretching, remember to stand up as it allows you to both stretch legs and arms.

**TYPES of Stretches**
•Static and Ballistic
•Use a static stretch, which is where you hold the stretch for a few seconds.

**Example Stretches:**
•Reach one arm across the other and then switch
•Touch the hands to the ground
•Roll your neck around in a circular motion

•Use of 18pt font is too small
•Times New Roman –instead use a Garamond or Arial

•Lacks a visual element that matches the message.

---

Each webinar platform allows for slides to be uploaded; however, some maintain the animation while others convert the slide into a still image. It's important to know in what way the information is taken into the platform before designing begins. How frustrating to take time creating awesome animations only to discover that they don't work during the webinar!

# POWERPOINT DESIGN PRINCIPLES

There are many books out there on PowerPoint design, and for every concept I will share, I am sure there are others who will come to a different conclusion. Keep in mind that designing slides for a classroom with ambient lighting or an auditorium with 3,000 people is not the same as PowerPoint with the sole purpose of being on a personal computer or laptop. When creating your slides for a webinar, the following tips can help your slides be more engaging and actually reduce the onset of headaches, which are common when staring at a computer screen for extended periods of time.

### BUILD IN WHITE SLIDES

When crafting your PowerPoint deck for synchronous training, insert slides in advance when you know there will be an exercise where the facilitator, producer and participants will be asked to write, draw or do a collaborative exercise. Although inserting a whiteboard on the fly is fairly simple, it is one less step to think about, and it helps to remind the facilitator that an interactivity is supposed to happen.

## UTILIZE DARK SLIDES WITH LIGHT WRITING

When participating in a webinar, notice the number of slides that are white background with dark words. On the flipside, using slides that are dark with light writing provides a distinct difference from the rest of the platform, which makes it easier for participants to differentiate the whiteboard area from the tools and other application areas of the platform. Why does the contrast matter?

Computer screens use pixels. Each pixel is a point of light on the computer screen that is very bright in the center and fades to nothing on the edges. If an optical muscle is repeatedly flexed over a long period of time, it can lead to a mix of eye and vision problems called Computer Vision Syndrome. It is also commonly believed that fatigued eye muscles lead to headaches, which can cause tension and then tight muscles in the neck, shoulder and back. One way I reduce the eye tension learners might experience is to limit the amount of bright light on the webinar platform and increase the amount of contrast and definition in images. Another way is to use bolded text and fewer words.

In general, I use slides with a white background for exercises when learners are unfamiliar with the writing tools and changing the color might just be too much for them. These sessions are typically 90 minutes or less.

A light background on slides makes it easier for participant interaction with the drawing tools like the use of color. When you're designing a slide, don't be tempted to choose just any background color because the choice is there; a bright background color or 50 colors doesn't necessarily make a slide more "visual." I recently had a client who used cotton candy pink as the PowerPoint deck background. In general, pink is not a color that should be used for a background. It should be used for things like ice cream and–you guessed it–cotton candy.

Background colors that are appropriate are blues, greens, blacks, deep purple (almost black), deep reds and grays. The text color should contrast sharply with the dark background. Typically that would include white, yellow, tan and most bright colors. Colors appropriate for highlighting are orange, yellow and most pastels.

## REDUCE WORDS

Use fewer words on your slides, but keep the meaning. Additional text can and should be in the handouts. This is not giving permission to have a thesis for a handout, merely explaining that slides should have limited words pre-designed. For example, I use pre-designed slides that have few words and then learners brainstorm their answers on the whiteboard. By the time we are done, there are a lot of words listed on the whiteboard; this is completely acceptable because the learners are participating and adding the extra content. The whiteboard they saw before the activity began was clean and simple.

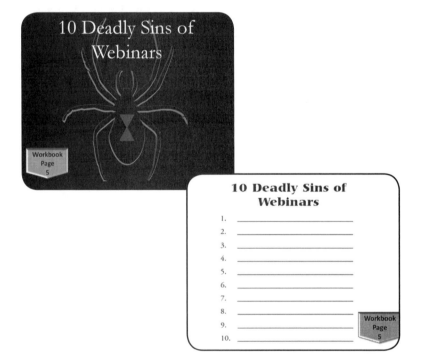

## REDUCE BULLETS

In 2003, Pulitzer-prize winning columnist Julia Keller wrote an article entitled, "Killing Me Microsoftly with PowerPoint." This would be an apt description of many webinars. The overuse of the program's many capabilities cloaks the actual content and inhibits communication. Line after line of text and slides riddled with bullet points and multiple fonts do not create retention. Nor do a plethora of continuous animation, 3-D charts and graphs that, frankly, would be easier to review if they were simple and one-dimensional.

Just because a tool has cool widgets and gadgets doesn't mean you have to use them all. Keep it simple and clean. When using animation, keep it discreet and consistent. This means if you have titles "fly in" from the right, be consistent and use the "fly in" animation for the rest of that slide. It isn't more creative to "fly in" for the first thought and then "box in" for the next.

Cut down the number of bullets you use by limiting yourself to one theme or idea per slide. Having one idea on each slide reduces confusion on the topic being covered, keeps the focus on a single topic and what you are saying, and keeps learners from jumping ahead.

## USE VISUAL LISTS

When you do decide a list of ideas will be an effective way of getting your message across, don't just create bulleted points. Try making the list more visual. For example, when creating an agenda for your learners, show your training itinerary as a road map with content signs along the side of the learning superhighway.

Here are two other examples of visual lists:

## CHOOSE APPROPRIATE FONTS

When we were selling our house, we repainted our daughter's razzle-dazzle rose room a sedate taupe so the color wouldn't overshadow the many features of the home. Just as home sellers try to remove distractions, so should webinar slide designers. Use these three text guidelines when creating your slides:

Use the 2x2 rule: keep to two fonts per slide and two sizes of font per slide. The title or subject line might be in a size 36 font while the body text might be size 32.

GET RID OF ALL CAPS. This is not only annoying and considered "yelling" in the world of social media, but it is also difficult to read. All caps should be saved for acronyms, word puzzles, acrostics and other special purposes.

Depending on the topic, different fonts might be appropriate for a slide or two. If having learners do an activity of unscrambling words, a SCRABBLE™ font would be creative and clever for that one slide but would not be appropriate for all slides within the session. Fonts that are easily readable in PowerPoint include Sans Serif fonts like Arial or Garamond. Fonts to avoid are Times New Roman and *Scripted* fonts. These fonts are more difficult for readers to view online because the letters are closer together. The contrast isn't as crisp, which can also increase eyestrain.

## INSERT PAGE NUMBERS ON SLIDES

When you are drafting your slides, simply add a subtle page number that corresponds with the page number in the handout. This will help learners who take an unscheduled break find where you are at and jump back into the learning without needing to ask another learner or the producer.

## BE CONSISTENT WITH TITLE SLIDES

Title slides should have the same title as what is in the workbook or handout. It is frustrating to listen to an instructor talk about a slide titled Change Management when the workbook page is labeled Managing Change in Corporate America. If you want to limit words, like a long title on the slides, make sure you use the same, shorter title in the handbook. Each graph should also have an identifying title or name so that learners know what it is about or where to locate it in the future.

## ADD VALUE BEYOND THE SLIDE

When teaching a synchronous class, only share need-to-know content. Slides, however, should accompany a handout. The handout has the need-to-know information, and the slides create a picture of what is being shared to more fully engage the learner by using another of the five senses. Slides should tell a story and allow the imagination to fill in the blanks.

## USE GRAPHICS THAT ENHANCE THE MESSAGE

When you use images, they need to take your content to the next level. If you are teaching about customer service, don't insert an irrelevant image of a character running because it's cute. Instead use a picture of you and your friends at Disney World. Why? Because Disney is known for its high level of commitment to great customer service. The image can now move your learners into a text chat about what comes to mind when you think of Disney World and customer service, and from there to messages your company wants to communicate about customer service.

## SLIDES SHOULD HAVE A CONCEPT

No matter how you design it, each slide should fit the context. The SCRABBLE word scramble is an example of this. That font creates an image in our minds. Even if a learner has never heard of SCRABBLE, the concept doesn't take away from the learning; it only enhances it for those who have had experience with the game. It provides a link to something they already know, which is a way to help people file information and increase retention. The more links one can make to prior knowledge and memories, the more memorable the learning.

## CREATE PRE-MADE QUESTION SLIDES

When you ask participants to interact by answering a question in some way, it is easier for them to do so if they can both hear and see the question. Often people get into their assigned breakout rooms and the first question they ask is, "What are we supposed to do?" They then spend the time trying to figure that out and are not brainstorming answers. To help avert this scenario and save precious time, have the question placed in each of the breakout rooms or in the main room to move the exercise along.

# POLLING

Because you can't see your learners during a webinar, you need to utilize other methods of gauging learner energy and motivation. Polling is a great and speedy way for the presenter to "see" what is going on with participants.

Different platforms have varying levels of polling capability. Some allow for multiple-choice polls and pacing while others may allow for only yes/no, check-mark and X-in-the-box responses. These tools were built into the platform to help monitor where learners are at with the content in regard to speed and understanding but also work nicely for creating quick quizzes to assess learning.

There are several ways to utilize the polling tool all throughout the webinar. Use it at the beginning to pre-test learners' knowledge of the topic or as a soft opener to have learners answer trivia or personal questions to begin community-building. You can also create surveys to determine interest in a topic or as a re-engagement technique merely by having participants indicate their feelings about the pace of a section.

When using this feature, know what polling and survey tools are available in your platform, whether or not you are able to share results immediately or in a delayed fashion, and if feedback is anonymous.

Below are some guidelines for how best to create and use polling for quiz questions, multiple-choice questions, matching items and post-testing.

## CREATING AND IMPLEMENTING QUIZ QUESTIONS

- Purposeless quiz questions are not a good use of webinar time. Make sure questions require higher-order cognition and not just merely fact recall. Don't ask "What does the 'C' in CORE stand for?" Instead, ask something like "Which of the following is an example of a closer?" The second question makes the learner look for what principles apply to a closer while the first merely requires recall.

- I would also suggest writing quiz questions section by section. Good quizzes are difficult to write, and the task is best done one at a time.
- Let learners know if guessing on a question is acceptable or if they should select "do not know" as the answer. This is especially key if you are doing a pre-test and want to know exactly where the group is at. For the post-test, determine whether the same rules apply.
- Use a visual timer to show the amount of time for each question or let learners know how long the poll will stay open. Also, let them know if answers can be changed or if it stays selected once it is chosen.

## MULTIPLE-CHOICE POLLING

- Express the full problem in the stem, or main statement. Make sure that participants can understand the problem before reading the alternative answers. Usually, direct questions are clearer than sentence completions.
- Put all relevant material in the stem. Do not repeat phrases in the options if the phrase can be stated in the stem.
- Keep the stem short. Unnecessary information confuses participants and wastes their time.
- Make the incorrect answers plausible. Incorrect answers should represent errors commonly made by participants. The best wrong answers are either too general or too specific; accurate but do not fully meet the requirements of the problem; or statements that appear correct. Avoid words that are too extreme such as "always," "never," "all" or "none" as few ideas or situations are absolute or universally true. On occasion, I have found that inserting a humorous incorrect answer lets participants laugh, which reduces tension which increases retention.
- Limit the number of optional answers. Robert Frary, in his book *Practical Assessment, Research & Evaluation*, provides a few facts on drafting multiple-choice questions.
  - o Having three answer options is about as effective as four choices.
  - o A four-response answer format is the most popular.
  - o Never give participants more than five alternatives.

o Never have both "None of the above" and "All of the above" as options for a single question.

- Do use "None of the above" as the final option, especially if the answer requires computation. Its use makes the question harder and more discriminating, because the uncertain student cannot focus on a set of options that must contain the answer.
- Make all choices similar in structure and equal in length. Do not give away the best choice by making it longer or more detailed.
- Avoid trick questions and double negatives. Negative phrasing often confuses and makes items unnecessarily complex. This also makes a question more challenging for English Speakers of Other Languages (ESOL) participants beyond what is necessary.
- Avoid typos and watch your grammar. Oftentimes we spend the most time scrutinizing the right answer and incorrect answers are quickly thrown together. When this happens, we may not be as careful with our grammar or typing in both the stem and the answers because they were more quickly added.
- Vary the position of the best answer. Research shows faculty tend to locate the best answer in the B or C position. Instead, use a deck of cards to locate correct responses randomly. For example, if you pull a heart, put the correct answer in the first position. Draw a spade? Place the answer in B, and so on.
- Keep the test length manageable. From Joseph Lowman's book *Mastering the Techniques of Teaching*, we know participants can only complete between one and two multiple-choice items per minute. Use that information to calculate how much time you'll need for your polling.

## MATCHING TEST ITEMS

- Give clear instructions. Let participants know how items are to be matched, where to write answers and whether a response may be used more than once.
- Keep the two sets of items homogeneous. For example, Column 1 may list events and Column 2 may list dates; do not combine events, dates and names in one column.
- Try to order the responses. If you order the items in Column

2 alphabetically, chronologically or conceptually, participants will be able to read the series more quickly and locate answers more rapidly than if there is no order.

- Create more responses than premises. In general, give participants five to 10 alternatives in Column 2. If you include distracters in Column 2, let participants know that some of the entries in Column 2 do not apply.
- Be conscious of the layout and format. Always keep both columns on the same page so that participants don't have to flip back and forth. Place answer blanks to the left of each entry in Column 1. Place Column 2 on the right-hand side of the page. Use capital letters for the responses (they are easier to discern than lowercase letters) and numbers for the premises.

### POST-TEST ITEM ANALYSIS
- Use the results to improve your tests. If everyone in the class is getting a quiz question wrong, think about revising or rewording the question. If the question is too difficult or too easy, think about throwing it out and creating a new one that will be more fair.
- Solicit participants' comments about the test.

# PARTICIPANT HANDOUTS

As I was preparing a handout for a conference presentation, I noticed a survey in my email inbox asking whether or not I could do my session at that conference without handouts. After I responded, I received an email from this organization stating they would not be printing handouts in an effort to go green. I got riled up and decided I would print my own. A handout is a critical tool for engagement and can assist the trainer in meeting the various visual and kinesthetic needs of learners.

Handouts also provide a way for learners to work on their own for a short time, which meets the needs of the reflective learner. Being a part of an interactive webinar is great for the active and participative learner, but the reflective learner needs time to absorb, process and work alone. By designing handouts that allow for independent study, you are recognizing the needs of all types of learners.

People in general are highly visual. That tendency can help bridge the comprehension gap left by an auditory message and bring learners to a conclusion much quicker. In the book *Made to Stick*, Chip and Dan Heath point out concrete concepts are more memorable than abstract. Handouts can help bring abstract ideas into a more concrete or clear message, thus making it easier to learn and remember.

## HANDOUT PRINCIPLES

- Don't use a copy of your PowerPoint deck as your handout. If your slides are designed well and your webinar is truly participant-centered, it wouldn't do the learner much good anyway. If you do not have time to modify your deck right away, at the very minimum, remove some of the words and replace them with a blank line for learners to fill in.
- Follow the same 2x2 principle as for PowerPoint design. Designers should keep to two fonts and two sizes of font per page. Too many fonts and font sizes distract the participant from the message being shared. Remember to keep it clean.
- Make your handouts interactive. The human brain likes completion. When someone starts a task and gets interrupted, the brain continues to search for completion. When there is a fill-in-the-blank on a page, most people, whether they are note-takers or not, want that blank filled in and will look for the right words in order to fulfill that subconscious need. If a facilitator skips the fill-in, many learners will be quietly annoyed and will try to figure out a word that makes sense. Oftentimes they will raise their virtual hand and ask for the answer to that missing blank.
- Use clear images that match the message and have a clean look and feel. This helps to draw learners into the workbook. When a page is disorganized or cluttered, participants will regularly look away and throw it away after the session.
- Number the pages. In writing this book, I printed off drafts not once but twice without page numbers and had no idea where I was at or what page to direct one of my editors to. It takes a lot more time to find something when there isn't a clear way to get to it. And if handouts aren't numbered, they won't match

the slide deck page number. It's a detail easily overlooked, and it's much easier to find a page by number than by title.

- Divide your handout into sections. At the very least, create a "need-to-know" section and an appendix. If you have a large workbook, think about using tabs for easy reference or have learners create and insert their own tabs. One of my first Bibles had a tab for each book. It was much quicker to find one of the 66 books before I memorized them. And, because your learners most likely won't be memorizing where chapters are, tabs make sense.
- Send out handouts in advance of the session. Let learners print off the workbook and be ready for the class to begin. Sending a large file the day of the event can cause many frustrations and headaches, and tempts Murphy's Law.
- The appendices of this book model several good handouts with job aids, charts, grids and reference material to aid in learning. You could also insert in-home study or project work as well as flow charts and marketing collateral. Having the information up close and personal can help when a slide just isn't big enough.

# CHAPTER FOUR

## TOOL OVERVIEW

If I were to poke my head under the hood of my minivan with monkey wrench and crowbar in hand, I'm sure my spouse would want some reassurance I knew what I was doing. While the physical mutilation might not be as dire online, you can cause a lot of collateral damage and create more work by not being familiar with the tools of your webinar platform. Here is a quick tutorial to get you started.

## APPLICATION SHARING

Application sharing has also been called remote desktop sharing and is a tool that is in almost every platform, whether for trainings or meetings. It functions as a way for people to view each other's desktop applications and collaborate on projects. Some platforms allow for all users to be able to host and share while others only allow for the moderator or facilitator to host. Application sharing is a great way to make learning meaningful because participants can immediately apply the content.

This tool is most commonly used to demonstrate software or navigate a website before the learner takes control and mirrors the process. This is good if you are hosting a webinar one-on-one or one-on-few because, in a large group, very few participants will get to "drive."

Application sharing can be a powerful tool if a little creativity is used. I really like playing games. Products like AllPlay Web and BRAVO! are two that allow learners to have a virtual response pad, and then the instructor application shares the actual game show and questions. This is a more advanced skill but a fun way to revisit content.

If you are drafting templates, application share the templates with the learner and together make annotations and modify the documents in real time. When sharing applications, it is critical to have a second computer logged in as a learner so that you are able to walk them around the screen and tell them where to look for information. Keep in mind that there are bandwidth differences and the amount of time it takes for one learner's page to refresh and redraw the screen could be up to a minute different from others.

A word of caution: when application sharing, be sure to close any private messages or confidential documents. You should also take the time to clear out cookies if application sharing the internet. Although I recommend using the synchronized web browsing to show items on the web, some platforms do not have this option, which means application-sharing is the alternative.

Five years ago, I was on a sales webinar, and the facilitator shared his desktop to show us improvements to a website. When he began typing the address into his web browser, a drop-down menu appeared showing several other website options that were clearly not for our eyes. I don't think it even crossed his mind because he just continued on. I have no idea what the rest of the call was about, because I was too busy laughing with the rest of the group.

Below are some questions to consider about your platform's application-sharing function before selecting activities to use from this book:

- Can you application-share a learner's desktop?
- Is the application-sharing view only for learners or can they interact with your desktop? What permissions are needed?
- How many learners can interact when an application is being shared?
- Can multiple applications be shared at one time? The entire desktop?
- What are the bandwidth requirements? How do I check to see if my learners are having trouble or how long the lag time is?
- Am I able to change control in the middle of application sharing?

# BREAKOUT ROOMS

I love using breakout rooms so smaller groups can work together and participate in a more intimate manner. Breakout rooms require everyone to either be engaged or feel like they are letting their group members down.

Breakout rooms, for the most part, are a more advanced tool. I didn't begin using this function until I felt I had mastered other tools because breakout rooms incorporate several of the other tools: whiteboard, text chat and audio. Those things alone triple the challenge for the end user.

Breakout rooms are great for brainstorming, working on project work, developing concepts, promoting a sense of team through relay races and competitions or splitting out of a larger group to connect with your smaller territory, pyramid or job function. When participants have an application time built into the class, which I highly recommend, a personal breakout room allows each learner to post ideas on a personal whiteboard to later report back insights and ideas. I have also used these to connect with my producer while learners are on a break so we can plan the next segment without the whole class listening in.

I have learned it is best to announce that we'll be moving into breakout rooms a few moments before actually doing so to allow the producer time to be ready so she can quickly move learners into the rooms. You may want to have a slide in each breakout room with instructions on what they are to do, even if you've already verbalized the instructions.

For learners that do not have audio capabilities, I encourage them to sign in with their name and after it put "the silent." So it shows up "Dan the silent" so others and I know Dan's responses will be text chatted. This tip comes from hearing myself say too many times, "Joe, go ahead and turn on your mic and share XYZ," and wait only to have Joe text chat, "I don't have a microphone, remember?" When so many people are in a session, it is difficult to keep track of who has audio capabilities, and it makes breakout room work a lot easier when others know the situation. They expect to read Joe's responses.

Below are some questions to consider about your platform's breakout room function before selecting activities to use from this book:

- How many participants can be in a breakout room?
- How many breakout rooms are available for use? Is it limited?
- Can breakout rooms be created prior to participants logging in?
- Can learners be pre-assigned to a breakout room?
- Can slides be pre-posted in each of the breakout rooms?
- When in a breakout room, can participants text chat?
- Can whiteboards from the breakout room be posted in the main room or do they need to be application shared?
- When the session is being recorded, will breakout rooms be recorded as well or only the main room?
- Can a participant be moved from one breakout room to another?
- How do participants let the trainer know they have a question when in a breakout room?
- Will participants be able to hear each other once they are in their breakout rooms if you're using a conference bridge?
- Can music or videos be played in breakout rooms?

## POLLING

Polling is one of the easiest tools to use, and it is available in every platform to varying degrees. Some platforms have a lot of emoticons users can use while others are very simple and have only hand-raising and pacing features. Polling can be interspersed and done quickly so it becomes a very attractive engagement tool, but it also is one of the most overused tools.

Polling can be used in soft openers and openers as the class begins. It is also a way to receive immediate feedback on session material. At the end of the session, it can be used for evaluations and can be either anonymous or public. More information on designing polling questions can be found in chapter 3.

Below are some questions to consider about your platform's polling function before selecting activities to use from this book:
- What polling options are available?
- Can the results be anonymous?
- Can polls be posted to the whiteboard?
- Is there a limit to the number of polls that can be done?
- Can questions be pre-designed or posted in the moment?
- Which polling options can export a report and be saved?
- Do survey results export by learner for testing purposes?

## TEXT CHAT

The text chat feature is just what you might guess it to be: a small box in the corner in which participants, producers or facilitators can type. When the enter key is hit, the statement, question or comment shows up in the public feed for all to see.

I personally prefer to always have the "chat room" open and allow learners to interact throughout the session. It is an easy way for learners to stay engaged, even on their own, and encourages a sense of community. From time to time, the comments may be about something else, but at least you know they are actively participating in the session and still online. The only time I would recommend limiting the text chat feature is if participants are abusing the tool and being inappropriate with their comments.

When learners are asked to text chat their thoughts, be sure to read the thoughts aloud when working with smaller class sizes or purposefully give them time to review their classmates' responses if it is a larger class. This affirms their thoughts and also makes their efforts seem worthwhile. If neither of these two things happens, learners stop participating because they feel like no one cares and that the activity is pointless.

Below are some questions to consider about your platform's text chat function before selecting activities to use from this book:

- Is private text chat available for learners to privately work in pairs?
- If private text chat is available, can the producer and trainer view those messages?
- Can hyperlinks be pasted into the chat area and still be live?
- Can participants copy and paste from the text chat area onto the whiteboard and vice-versa?
- Is text chat limited to a certain number of people at a time or is group text chat available?
- Can access to text chatting be limited by participant?
- Can participants view main room text chats in their breakout rooms?
- If a learner logs in late, will she be able to view a history of text chats?
- Can the text chat history and log be saved and viewed later?
- Is there a limit to the length of characters in the text chat area?

## TWO-WAY AUDIO

When doing webinars, think about all the ways you can use audio so that you are not the only one talking and straining your voice. For me, the biggest difference between a live classroom and an online classroom was how much talking I did online. Although learners were engaging, I found myself doing more of the announcing of text chats or thoughts on the whiteboard. Having a lot of water nearby helps from drying out and cracking, but hearing my own voice for hours got a bit monotonous for me and the learners.

Listening to a new voice is one way to re-engage a learner, and it is easy to do. Try bringing in learners and letting them share their ideas out loud. They are able to expound on their idea, and it builds a connection to that person. A participant vocalizing how content will be applied also increases his retention of the information.

Keep in mind that two-way VoIP audio can also have lag time for learners, and it is always a good idea to have a back-up plan for the session. Talking too fast or too slow can make learners wonder if there is something wrong. Do your best to use pauses for impact, not for finding your place. Pretend you are a talk-show host. Show enthusiasm and excitement as well as passion through your voice. Do what you would do in the classroom: call on learners, use team leaders to share back with the group, speak at a comfortable pace and use word pictures to describe content. Keep in mind that there is regularly a bit of lag time between you speaking and listeners hearing, so wait for learners to respond before talking again.

To reduce feedback, have learners push their on-off microphone icon. Only the person sharing should have their microphone on. If a learner wants to comment, teach them to raise their hand so they can be called on to avoid talking over one another. Unlike conference calls, multiple talkers can't be heard at the same time with VoIP.

Below are some questions to consider about your platform's audio function before selecting activities to use from this book:
- Can all learners turn on their microphones and have permissions?
- Does my platform allow for both VoIP and a conference call to be used simultaneously if learners are having streaming problems?
- If learners are on a conference call connected to the platform, can they share when they are in breakout rooms?
- If a learner doesn't have a headset, can they still talk without feedback coming through?

## VIDEO

Because of the large file sizes, the video tool is one of the most challenging for most platforms; however, a few platforms have found ways to stream video quicker and better, and it is amazing how far this feature has come.

Most platforms only support webcam streaming and not actual video-sharing because of bandwidth issues. If that is the case for your platform, think about housing a video on your website and sharing the link so that learners can view at their own streaming pace. Try to reduce the file size so slower computer systems can more quickly access and play the file.

If you have a platform that does stream video, practice and prepare timing and gauge how it will work for learners if they have VoIP versus a conference call line. If the conference call is not connected to the webinar platform, the sound may not work.

Below are some questions to consider about your platform's video function before selecting activities to use from this book:
- Does my platform support video feed?
- What are the requirements for users to view the video?
- What codec or player plug-in is needed?
- What resolution is the best for streaming a webcam on my platform?
- Can still pictures from a webcam be taken and shown on the screen so the webcam can be turned off and the image discussed?
- How many webcams can be viewed at a time and what are the bandwidth requirements surrounding multiple webcams being on?

## WEB BROWSING AND TOURS

Take your class on a field trip to the world wide web using this tool! If planning is done in advance, a trainer can take learners to a web page and have them search for the missing answers in their handouts; with the click of a button, everyone is there. Pretty cool stuff!

Those in sales and marketing have used this tool to its fullest; so much learning can happen by viewing websites and examples for discussion.

If you want to use an interactive word search and have participants do it on their own, this is the tool to use. Any flash-based, internet-hosted game can be launched in this manner for learners. Keep in mind that web addresses can work and then break. Make sure they are working the day of the session, and take into account the sites that are being visited. If a site requires a password or is blocked by an organization, the tour may come to an abrupt halt. Prevent this by having various users test the link and see if they are able to access it from their work computer.

Below are some questions to consider about your platform's web browsing and tours function before selecting activities to use from this book:

- What plug-ins and codecs are needed for learners to view content?
- What happens once I get to the website? Do learners have control of their desktops, or can I direct them to follow me?
- Can learners have control of the web tour and select the sites?
- Can learners navigate away from the browsing tour?
- Can each learner use their default browser or do they all have to use the same browser?
- Can hyperlinks and bookmarks be created in advance and used?
- If on a site that is firewalled for some learners, what happens? Is there a workaround?
- What permissions do learners need to have prior to the class?
- Are there bandwidth issues to consider?

## WHITEBOARD

The whiteboard, a multifaceted tool, is the most commonly used tool for a trainer or facilitator because it "houses" the slides that were created. It acts as both the projector as well as your flip chart in the online classroom. If you would normally create a flip chart in the moment, the same would be done in the session, as long as you are able to talk and write at the same time.

Use the whiteboard for directions, collaboration, visual support and engagement. When creating slides, think about which ones are for support and which ones learners will be writing or drawing on. For learners with little webinar experience, it is easiest to only have to find the text tool and write, and not worry about changing font size or color.

The whiteboard allows for creativity and imagination. It is fun to watch learners get creative in how they use their tools to post their thoughts.

Below are some questions to consider about your platform's whiteboard function before selecting activities to use from this book:

- How many participants can annotate on the whiteboard at a time?
- Can you upload slides prior to the session?
- Can all documents be uploaded to the whiteboard or just slide decks?
- What tools can be used? (e.g. highlighter, text, drawing, insert images, lines and shapes, and pointer tools.)
- Can you see all uploaded slides and jump ahead or go back when needed without clicking through all the slides?
- Does the slide import as a JPEG or does it maintain its flash and animated components?
- Can words and images be moved around on the slide?
- Can whiteboard slides created by the group be saved and exported for further discussion?
- Can breakout room whiteboard slides be moved over to the main room?
- Can permission for tools be turned on and off during the session?
- Can drawings and graphics be erased or removed?
- Do whiteboards maintain their annotations even after moving on to another slide?

# CHAPTER FIVE

## TYPES OF INTERACTIVITIES AND HOW TO USE THEM

You never get a second chance to make a good first impression. How you handle log-in difficulties, open the webinar, or help those struggling to get up to speed all impact each learner's first impression of your online training session.

A participant-centered webinar uses different types of interactions to help make the first, last and every impression along the way positive and lasting. By utilizing CLOSER (Closers, Learning activities, Openers, Soft openers, Energizers and Revisiters), you are choosing to put WoW Factor into your webinars. Participants aren't used to being engaged through entire webinars. When they experience an interactive one with better recall of the material covered, they leave delighted and look more positively toward the next one.

**WEBINAR LENGTH:** 60 minutes or longer
**ACTIVITY LENGTH:** Varies
**INSTRUCTOR SKILL LEVEL:** Novice
**PARTICIPANT SKILL LEVEL:** Novice
**SUPPLIES:** Slide, 2-4 content cards per person
**TOOLS:** Two-way Audio, Whiteboard

CLOSER
**LEARNING ACTIVITY**
OPENER
SOFT OPENER
ENERGIZER
**REVISITER**

### CARD MATCH

**PURPOSE:** Apply Material, Familiarizing, Preview Material, Recall Background Knowledge, Recall Information-Existing Schemas, Review

The last section of this book lays out more than 40 activities you can do in a webinar to keep people engaged and motivated while still focusing on your content. Following is a brief tutorial on what the purpose of each part of CLOSER is so you can easily select the right activities from the last chapter for your content segments.

## CLOSERS

Think about the last webinar you were on. What were the last five minutes like? Did the instructor do a question-and-answer time? Did it go long? Did the instructor ask for an evaluation to be filled out?

The last few minutes of a session is prime real estate and should be used for information to be solidified and branded on the brain. People should walk away knowing what their next action step is and how to get started with that.

A closer can be motivational and inspirational. Closers revisit the content and bring things full circle. They are a chance to celebrate and rejoice in the learning and be proud of what has been accomplished. If learners walk away feeling poorly about how much they don't know, we have done a great disservice to them.

The course evaluation should not be part of the closer. Evaluations should be done about three-fourths of the way through the training so the last minutes can be focused on the learners and what they are taking away.

When selecting a closer, pick one that suits the time frame—the shorter the class, the shorter the closer. I usually have a backup closer just in case I was planning on having 10 minutes, but now we are down to 3 minutes. Even in 3 minutes, I can do a quick whiteboard close. There are several ideas in this book that are shorter in time frame and others can be modified for a quicker close as well.

## LEARNING ACTIVITY

Many instructional designers find it easy to adapt to using an opener and a closer; however, most find it challenging to take the content and make it more interactive. Learning activities are the interactive framework on which to hang your content.

For example, a learning frame could be as simple as using a card match or sort. Take a section of your information, like a step-by-step process. Create cards with the information on them, with one complete or partial step per card. Have six to 12 cards per slide, then have learners review the deck and highlight what they think goes first. When someone has identified and explained what additional information is needed, move on to the next. Instead of a bulleted PowerPoint lecture, the content has become active, and learners are engaged as they automatically want to know if their guess or deduction was right.

While learning through these activities usually takes longer than a lecture, they also incorporate case studies, brainstorming and information application. Learning activities are the "lecture" because you are teaching as you go through the activity.

## OPENERS

When starting a training session, you need to first break learner preoccupation for your information to have the best chance of sticking. Openers are your first line of offense for this task.

Openers can serve many purposes, including creating an atmosphere of collegiality. These activities get people into the room, get them networking and make the session feel more like a real class, and not just solitary confinement. They can decrease tension in a group and provide a safe way to practice using the tools and talking with others. When one person begins sharing, others feel more comfortable opening up. Soon all participants are text chatting, and there is a bit of relief as tool-usage confidence is built as are relationships. Openers lay the groundwork for participation throughout the rest of the webinar.

The length of the opener depends on the amount of content used and the length of the session. If there are four 3-hour modules, I will spend about 30 minutes opening the first day to lay the foundation for a safe environment. This way, when I later engage them in a rather off-the-wall energizer, the participants participate as I model the exercise via my webcam.

As you read through the different interactivities at the end of this book, some can be used as the opener or closer because they meet the principles of both.

# SOFT OPENERS

Soft openers help warm up the brain and get it going. Strong soft openers will encourage lateral thinking, meaning it is both creative and logical, requiring both sides of the brain to come up with a solution. Good soft openers should tie into the content, but not be need-to-know. They are meant to be an add-on and should transition into the opener. They should also be simple and allow for all learners to join in.

Soft openers are typically started 5 to 10 minutes before beginning the webinar and engage the audience, set the tone, put attendees at ease and allow learners to begin practicing the platform tools.

My producer and I welcome people as they enter the session and have them chat with us for a minute. A warm welcome with a question after is a simple way to break the ice and start a conversation. Then we'll start the soft opener.

If the group is new to one another, use the soft opener to connect people or find out what they already know about the training topic. If the participants are from all different levels of the organization, you could use the soft opener to level out the playing field—no matter what role you have, all are equal when it comes to whiteboarding how you feel right now or text chatting a solution to a puzzle.

The soft opener ideas in this book just need your content. I typically finish up the final soft opener about 3 minutes into the session so everyone can finish logging in. I then move into the opener. Soft openers only occur prior to the start of a session. They are not mandatory but they are part of what creates a WoW Factor.

# ENERGIZERS

When you are feeling tired, your learners are as well. Do a quick energizer and watch yourself transform! You and your learners will feel better.

Energizers are activities that get the blood flowing and help participants refocus. If you don't have a few energizers ready and planned into your webinar, they are unlikely to happen. The most useful times for energizers in a webinar tend to be after a large section of content or application practice around the 60-minute mark. If you are hosting a webinar after lunch, a quick break about 20 minutes into your session is a good time to get people back on their feet for a physical energizer to increase blood flow and oxygen for optimal brain function and learning.

Energizers are the one type of activity that do not have to specifically relate to the content. Energizers are meant to be a rapid way to get learners re-engaged. The energizers in this book are 1 to 5 minutes. When you decide to use a longer energizer, consider a revisiter that has a kinesthetic component.

# REVISITERS

What on earth is a revisiter and is it contagious? A revisit activity is similar to a review in that it goes over content already covered; however, review is where the instructor goes over the material again. A revisit is where the learner goes over the material. Some of the main differences between the two are listed in Chart 5.1. There is a time and place for both, but a revisiter will usually benefit the learner more and provide a growing action plan.

| CONVENTIONAL REVIEW | PARTICIPANT-CENTERED REVISIT |
|---|---|
| Announce the review | Don't announce, just do it |
| Trainer does a summary | Learners summarize |
| Specific right or wrong answers | Flexible answers |
| Conceptual in nature [This is how it will work] | Behavioral [This is how I will apply it] |
| Test based | Journal and internal discovery |
| Fixed structure | Unstructured |
| Measurable | More difficult to measure |
| Examples: PowerPoint review slides, verbal review, reading review, observation with note taking, theoretical work | Examples: Physical activity, games and exercises, actually doing the job or task with a job aid, teaching others, top takeaway, brainstorming/journaling |

*Chart 5.1*

Chapter 6 is designed to save trainers time by providing easy, ready-to-use exercises. These exercises are cross-referenced in the index. Keep in mind that activity lengths can last longer than the length specified depending on the number of participants, complexity of the content and the amount of application time a trainer wants to provide.

Most exercises require a slide be made in advance; however, it is better to be using the exercises, even if you don't have time to create the appropriate slide using PowerPoint design principles for webinars.

Each of the activities in this book also has a slide created with the design principles in mind. To save time and avoid slide-design frustration, these slides can be purchased on WebinarsWithWow Factor.com for about the price of a good Chicago-style pizza.

Congratulations on taking steps to make your webinars more engaging. I look forward to seeing you in a live online session!

Good luck and God bless,

*Becky Pluth*

# CHAPTER SIX

## INTERACTIVITIES

**WEBINAR LENGTH:** Any

**ACTIVITY LENGTH:** 10-15 minutes

**INSTRUCTOR SKILL LEVEL:** Novice

**PARTICIPANT SKILL LEVEL:** Intermediate

**SUPPLIES:** Slide

**TOOLS:** Group Whiteboard, Two-way Audio

CLOSER
LEARNING ACTIVITY
OPENER
SOFT OPENER
ENERGIZER
REVISITER

# AROUND THE WORLD

**PURPOSE:** Brainstorm, Establish a Learning Community, Familiarizing, Recall Background Knowledge, Recall Information-Existing Schemas, Refocus Learner, Review

## SET-UP

- Create a slide that includes the following:
    - o  Title: Around the World
    - o  Insert faint colorful watermark image of nature or the world
- Insert the slide(s) into the presentation at the appropriate place based on your purpose: in the beginning as an opener, partway through the webinar if used as a revisiter, or before a break or at the very end of the session if used as a closer. If used as a learning activity, insert the slide when the content comes up in the presentation.

## TRAINER PROCESS

- Put up the "Around the World" slide.
- Have each participant write their name on the whiteboard in a color that will show up against the background.
- Each participant will have a turn to share on the topic you

name. It could be a best learning, step in a process or a solution to a problem.

- Virtually hand the highlighter to a first participant, and tell them you're handing off the koosh ball. They will share a first idea and "toss" the virtual koosh ball to another name on the whiteboard by drawing a line from their name to another.
- This continues until everyone has shared.

## PRODUCER PROCESS

- In a document, keep track of brainstorming ideas shared.
- Help learners with tools and drawing lines if needed.
- Make sure microphones are muted after each share.

## VARIATIONS

- In a hurry? Sometimes drawing the line takes up a bit of time. Use a pointing tool instead of the highlighter and point at the next person to share.
- Shorten the activity by allowing learners to only share one word or one sentence before passing the baton.

**WEBINAR LENGTH:** Any

**ACTIVITY LENGTH:** 5 minutes

**INSTRUCTOR SKILL LEVEL:** Intermediate

**PARTICIPANT SKILL LEVEL:** Intermediate

**SUPPLIES:** Slide

**TOOLS:** Group Whiteboard

CLOSER
LEARNING ACTIVITY
**OPENER**
SOFT OPENER
ENERGIZER
**REVISITER**

| | |
|---|---|
| A | N |
| B | O |
| C | P |
| D | Q |
| E | R |
| F | S |
| G | T |
| H | U |
| I | V |
| J | W |
| K | X |
| L | Y |
| M | Z |

# ATZRR
## (A TO Z RELAY RACE)

**PURPOSE:** Brainstorm, Establish a Learning Community, Familiarizing, Recall Background Knowledge, Recall Information-Existing Schemas, Refocus Learner, Review

## SET-UP

- Create a handout titled "Top Takeaways" for participants to write down learnings throughout the webinar.
- Create a slide that includes the following:
  - o A to Z Relay
  - o Split the slide into two halves with the letters A-M running vertically down the left hand side and the letters N-Z down the middle of the page with one letter per line. All the letters of the alphabet (English or otherwise) should be listed out.
- Insert the slide(s) into the presentation at the appropriate place based on your purpose: in the beginning as an opener, part-way through the webinar if used as a revisiter or, if used as a closer, before a break or at the very end of the session.

## TRAINER PROCESS

- Have learners turn to their "Top Takeaways" page.
- Put up the "A to Z Relay" slide.

- Split group into two teams.
- Each participant on a team will select a different color with which to write. Players must rotate who is writing. For example, the learner who selected green writes down A-action ideas. That learner must then wait for a teammate to post another idea before they may post again. Thus the relay!
- Learners will fill in each letter with a learning point from the session. In a customer service class you might see P=Positive Attitude, S=Smile on the phone, X=Xtra time with elderly, etc. Share with participants that creative spelling counts!
- When a group is done, all participants raise their virtual hand and the game is over!
- Before starting the relay, ask if anything needs clarifying.
- Check in on participants in their breakout rooms during the relay (variation only).
- When completed, discuss the ideas as a large group.
- Direct learners to add ideas to their "Top Takeaways" page.
- Have learners then circle their favorite idea posted on the whiteboard.

# PRODUCER PROCESS

- Put up a timer for 30, 45 or 60 seconds and have it count down (variation only).
- Post A to Z slide in breakout rooms (variation only).
- After groups are done, post the winning slide in the main room (variation only).

# VARIATIONS

- Depending on the size of the class you can work as a large group on the main room whiteboard.
- If a large group, put the A to Z chart in each breakout room and race against other breakout rooms to finish the entire chart first. The team that finishes first and raises their hands wins.
- If it is a small group, make it a relay race against the clock to see who wins.
- If it is a small group, have one team work on the first half of the alphabet while the other group works on the second half.

**WEBINAR LENGTH:** Any

**ACTIVITY LENGTH:** 10-15 minutes

**INSTRUCTOR SKILL LEVEL:** Advanced

**PARTICIPANT SKILL LEVEL:** Intermediate

**SUPPLIES:** Slide, Hyperlink for Response Pads

**TOOLS:** Application Share, Two-way Audio, Virtual Response Pad

**CLOSER**
**LEARNING ACTIVITY**
**OPENER**
**SOFT OPENER**
**ENERGIZER**
**REVISITER**

# BRAVO!™
## WITH PING™ VIRTUAL RESPONSE SYSTEM

**PURPOSE:** Apply Material, Brainstorm, Combining, Establish a Learning Community, Familiarizing, Innovate New Ideas, Introduce New Concept, Preview Material, Recall Background Knowledge, Recall Information-Existing Schemas, Refocus Learner, Review, Teach New Material

## SET-UP

- Purchase BRAVO! With PING software or download a trial license for free at C3Softworks.com
- Select an interactive game that suits the content. All the games are colorful and fully customizable. For fun, create a custom avatar that looks like the president of the company as one of the contestants.
- Create and test the game.
- Insert PING link into leader's guide for quick reference.
- Create a slide that includes the following:
    - o Image of the launch page and image of the response pad.
    - o Directions on how the game works. This will vary based on the exercise selected by the facilitator.
    - o Link to the PING pad.

# TRAINER PROCESS

- Put up the slide of the image and directions for learners.
- Split learners into groups based on the number of teams desired.
- Launch BRAVO! game on facilitator desktop to get ready for application share.
- Have learners click on the hyperlink. Let them know a new window will open when they click on the link. This new window can be moved around so that they are still able to see the facilitator's screen and platform.
- Once the window pops up, click on the Launch button.
- Wait for learners while they do this.
- Have learners select their team and enter their name.
- Watch as learners' names begin to ring in. Once all have rung in, start application sharing the game.
- Start the game and ask the questions. Have participants ring in with their virtual PING pads.
- Continue getting answers to game questions until the game is done.
- Stop application sharing and have learners text chat learnings from the exercise.

# PRODUCER PROCESS

- Help participants get up and running with the PING virtual pads.
- Monitor text chat area while game is in play.

# VARIATIONS

- Application share BRAVO! without the PING pads and have learners raise their hand or text chat the letter as their response.
- Have learners go through their own version.

**WEBINAR LENGTH:** > 90 minutes

**ACTIVITY LENGTH:** 20-30 minutes

**INSTRUCTOR SKILL LEVEL:** Advanced

**PARTICIPANT SKILL LEVEL:** Advanced

**SUPPLIES:** Slide

**TOOLS:** Breakout Rooms, Group Whiteboard

CLOSER

LEARNING ACTIVITY

**OPENER**

SOFT OPENER

ENERGIZER

**REVISITER**

# BURSTING BALLOONS

**PURPOSE:** Apply Material, Combining, Establish a Learning Community, Familiarizing, Innovate New Ideas, Introduce New Concept, Preview Material, Recall Background Knowledge, Recall Information-Existing Schemas, Refocus Learner, Review, Teach New Material

## SET-UP

- Create a handout titled "Top Takeaways" for participants to write down learnings throughout the webinar.
- Create a slide that includes the following:
    - o Title: Bursting Balloons
    - o An image in the background of multicolored balloons that are labeled with topics covered in the session.
    - o Team moderator is the person wearing the most colors.
- Insert the slide(s) into the presentation at the appropriate place based on your purpose: in the beginning as an opener, part-way through the webinar if used as a revisiter or, if used as a closer, before a break or at the very end of the session.

## TRAINER PROCESS

- Have learners turn to their "Top Takeaways" page.
- Put up the "Bursting Balloons" slide.
- Split the group into two teams.

- Share that groups will be put into breakout rooms in just a moment and that each group is to write concepts on the white board that relate to each topic on the balloons.
- Demonstrate by writing an idea on the whiteboard.
- Set the timer for 2 minutes. Encourage learners to list as many ideas on their whiteboards as they can for each topic.
- After 2 minutes, teams will highlight their top two ideas and meet back in the main room
- Ask, "What questions can I answer regarding this activity?"
- Send groups into their assigned breakout rooms for 2 minutes.
- Return teams to the main room.
- Note: If doing this as an opener, do this as a large group in the main room. Have learners list things they already know about the topics to be covered today.
- Have team leader share best two ideas with the large group. No repeats.
- Have participants add to their "Top Takeaways" page in their workbooks while groups are sharing.

## PRODUCER PROCESS

- Create breakout rooms.
- Post the "Balloon Burst" slide in each breakout room.
- Send learners into their breakout rooms.
- Put up a timer for 2 minutes and have it count down.
- Check in on breakout rooms and answer any questions.
- Post breakout room whiteboards into the main room for viewing or application share the whiteboards.
- Tally the number of points each team receives and post the score on their slide.

## VARIATIONS

- If it is a small group, each participant can be on their own team or work as a large group to achieve a certain score in 2 minutes.
- If working on a platform that allows for animation, create hyperlinks and allow learners to click on a balloon, which will then reveal the topic. Groups can share via text chat what they have learned.

**69**

**WEBINAR LENGTH:** 60 minutes or longer

**ACTIVITY LENGTH:** Varies

**INSTRUCTOR SKILL LEVEL:** Novice

**PARTICIPANT SKILL LEVEL:** Novice

**SUPPLIES:** Slide, Two to Four Content Cards Per Person

**TOOLS:** Two-way Audio, Whiteboard

CLOSER
**LEARNING ACTIVITY**
OPENER
SOFT OPENER
ENERGIZER
**REVISITER**

# CARD MATCH

**PURPOSE:** Apply Material, Familiarizing, Preview Material, Recall Background Knowledge, Recall Information-Existing Schemas, Review

## SET-UP

- Prior to the session, create a deck of cards. Each card should be labeled with a piece of content covered in this session. Content could include terms or images depending on the session material.
- Determine the number of cards each person will receive. This can vary from two to four random cards per learner.
- If there are not enough content pieces for unique cards for each learner, you can repeat content cards as needed.
- Email or mail each participant two to four random cards (you may want to keep track of who received what pieces).
- Create "Card Match" revisit slide(s) that include the following:
  - o Title: "Card Match" with image of playing cards or the scanned-in cards that were created.
  - o The content of the slide(s) should match the cards created. For example, content could include terms or images depending on the session material.
- Insert pre-made "Card Match" revisit slide(s) in several places throughout the deck after a few content pieces have been covered. This is roughly every 20 minutes.

# TRAINER PROCESS

- At the beginning of the session, have participants open their cards and read or view their cards.
- Explain that each card correlates to content to be covered. At certain points along the way, you will stop and do a "card match." This is when anyone who has a card with a topic that was covered will raise their hand and share one thing they learned on the topic or how they plan to adapt, adopt and apply what they learned back on the job.
- Learners should take notes on their cards as the content is covered and be ready to share.
- Put up the "Card Match" slide.
- Have participants raise their hands if one of their cards has been covered.
- Call on each, one at a time, and have them share one thing they learned on that topic or how they plan to adapt, adopt and apply what they learned back on the job.

# PRODUCER PROCESS

- Participate as the radio show announcer reading the text chat or whiteboard ideas.

# VARIATION

- To speed up this exercise, have learners that raised their hands whiteboard or text chat their ideas and as a talk-show host "announce" their thoughts to the group or have another learner do so.
- If participants have prior knowledge or you want to include information learned in a prior session, add directions that some cards have content from the past sessions and that they can share how they have been applying it on the job.

71

**WEBINAR LENGTH:** > 30 minutes

**ACTIVITY LENGTH:** 2-5 minutes

**INSTRUCTOR SKILL LEVEL:** Novice

**PARTICIPANT SKILL LEVEL:** Novice

**SUPPLIES:** Slide

**TOOLS:** Group Whiteboard

CLOSER

LEARNING ACTIVITY

OPENER

SOFT OPENER

ENERGIZER

**REVISITER**

Chart Chase 1

# CHART CHASE

**PURPOSE:** Apply Material, Brainstorm, Combining, Establish a Learning Community, Familiarizing, Innovate New Ideas, Introduce New Concept, Preview Material, Recall Background Knowledge, Recall Information-Existing Schemas, Refocus Learner, Review, Teach New Material

## SET-UP

- Create a handout titled "Top Takeaways" for participants to write down learnings throughout the webinar.
- Create a slide that includes the following:
    o Title: Chart Chase
- Insert the slide throughout for revisiting or, if used as a closer, before a break or the end.

## TRAINER PROCESS

- Have learners turn to their "Top Takeaways" page.
- Put up the "Chart Chase" slide.
- Share that the group will have 30, 45 or 60 seconds to post as many learnings as possible. Select the time that best fits the number of ideas possible. The fewer the number of ideas the shorter the time. Keep in mind some learners are slow typers.

Learners new to the platform and using tools may also need more time. Assess the audience to determine the length of time.

- Post ideas on the whiteboard using the webinar platform tools (different colors, drawing tools, text, etc.).
- Duplicates do not count.
- The goal is to beat the last team's score. If this is the first time using this activity, have a goal of one to two ideas per person that are unique or take the number of learning points and divide by two. Don't be surprised by the number of unique ideas a group can generate in such a short amount of time.
- When time is up, pause the group by saying, "Time's up, pens up. It is now time to add ideas to your 'Top Takeaways' page while I [or learners] read the whiteboard ideas and count the number of unique ideas."
- Have learners then star their favorite idea so far.

# PRODUCER PROCESS

- Put up a timer for 30, 45 or 60 seconds and have it count down.
- Answer any questions that come through via text chat.

# VARIATIONS

- Do this several times throughout a session trying to get the number posted higher and higher each time.
- Have learners post ideas on how to adapt the information to their work.
- Have learners post how they will adopt the information in the next month.

**WEBINAR LENGTH:** > 30 minutes

**ACTIVITY LENGTH:** 2-5 minutes

**INSTRUCTOR SKILL LEVEL:** Intermediate

**PARTICIPANT SKILL LEVEL:** Intermediate

**SUPPLIES:** Slide

**TOOLS:** Whiteboard and Drawing/Writing tools

CLOSER
LEARNING ACTIVITY
OPENER
SOFT OPENER
ENERGIZER
**REVISITER**

# CHART CHASE 2

**PURPOSE:** Brainstorm, Combining, Establish a Learning Community, Familiarizing, Innovate New Ideas, Introduce New Concept, Preview Material, Recall Background Knowledge, Recall Information-Existing Schemas, Refocus Learner, Review, Teach New Material

## SET-UP

- Create a handout titled "Top Takeaways" for participants to write down learnings throughout the webinar.
- Create a slide that includes the following:
    o Chart Chase 2
    o Split the slide into one quadrant per group; if there are only two groups, the slide will have a line down the middle creating a T. If there are four groups, it will look like a cross with four sections. Label each section Group 1, Group 2, etc.
- Insert the slides throughout for revisiting or before break or the end to be used as a closer.

## TRAINER PROCESS

- Have learners turn to their "Top Takeaways" page.
- Put up the "Chart Chase 2" slide.
- Split participants into two or four teams. Label each team Group

1, Group 2, etc. A quick way to split teams is alphabetically by first name.

- Share that the group will have 30 seconds (or other appropriate amount of time) to post as many learnings as possible. If learners are new to the webinar platform, it would be best to begin with the activity titled "Chart Chase" to reduce frustration.
- Each team has a designated section where they will post ideas on the whiteboard using the webinar platform tools (different colors, drawing tools, text, etc.).
- Once an idea has been called out, it is "taken" and cannot be repeated. The facilitator will call out ideas as they are posted.
- Learners compete against other teams to post the most learning points in a given amount of time. You can keep a running tally of points to award prizes.
- When time is up, pause the group by saying, "Time's up, pens up. It is now time to add ideas to your 'Top Takeaways' page while I count the number of unique ideas."
- Have learners then highlight their favorite idea so far on the whiteboard.

## PRODUCER PROCESS

- Put up a timer for the right amount of time and have it count down.
- Answer any questions that come through via text chat.
- Keep track of prize winners and send out awards.
- Ensure participants have permission to use their microphones or talk (variation only).

## VARIATIONS

- They raise their hand, turn on their mics and call out a topic and jot it in their space. Go in order of who raised their hand first.
- Keep a running tally of points throughout multiple session webinars and give away "bonus bucks" or online gift cards.
- Change up the award for the most ideas and keep your learners guessing.

WEBINAR LENGTH: > 90 minutes, multi-day
ACTIVITY LENGTH: 5-15 minutes
INSTRUCTOR SKILL LEVEL: Novice
PARTICIPANT SKILL LEVEL: Novice
SUPPLIES: Slide
TOOLS: Two-way Audio, Whiteboard

CLOSER
LEARNING ACTIVITY
OPENER
SOFT OPENER
ENERGIZER
REVISITER

# CHECK AND BALANCE

**PURPOSE:** Applying Material, Combining, Review

## SET-UP

- Create a "Top Takeaways" handout for the learners to add learnings to throughout the session.
- Create a "Check and Balance" slide that includes a picture of each participant or have each participant name listed.
- Insert the slide into the presentation at the end of the presentation as the final activity of the webinar.

## TRAINER PROCESS

- Put up the "Check and Balance" slide.
- Have learners open their books to a "Top Takeaways" notes page and take 60 seconds to jot down ideas they want to be sure and use.
- After 60 seconds, begin a large group discussion by highlighting a learner's name.
- Have that person turn on their microphone and then share their learning and how they will use it.

- After they are done sharing, they will highlight another learner's name.
- The trick is that none of the learnings can be repeated! This is one way to evaluate whether the key points were caught and remembered.
- If a participant's top idea is "taken," they can move down their list and share a different idea.

# PRODUCER PROCESS

- Put up timer for 60 seconds.
- Ensure learner microphone permissions are enabled.

# VARIATIONS

- Have learners post their idea next to their name.
- Assign topic areas to groups of learners to focus on.
- Add additional theory after participants share as needed.

**WEBINAR LENGTH:** Any

**ACTIVITY LENGTH:** 10-15 minutes

**INSTRUCTOR SKILL LEVEL:** Novice

**PARTICIPANT SKILL LEVEL:** Novice

**SUPPLIES:** Slide

**TOOLS:** Text Chat

CLOSER
**LEARNING ACTIVITY**
OPENER
SOFT OPENER
**ENERGIZER**
**REVISITER**

# CHIT CHAT

**PURPOSE:** Apply Material, Brainstorm, Familiarizing, Innovate New Ideas, Introduce New Concept, Recall Background Knowledge, Refocus Learner, Review

## SET-UP

- Create a slide that includes the following:
    - o  Watermark image of people chatting.
    - o  Titled "Chit Chat" with the following information listed: Using the Chat or Instant Message tool bar, Text Chat one fact or learning on ___ [facilitator to select the topic. Examples: Text chat your number one takeaway. Text chat one thing you look forward to doing this weekend. Text Chat how you will apply principle X on the job. Brainstorm different ways to use this information.]
- Insert the slide into the presentation at any point as an energizer.

## TRAINER PROCESS

- Put up the "Chit Chat" slide.
- Have learners stand up and stretch while they text chat the answer to the question.

- Turn on webcam to demonstrate standing up and model texting an idea.
- Once learners have finished answering, have them read through three other responses and then take their seats.
- Read a few answers out loud and comment as participants are typing up their thoughts.
- Turn off webcam.
- If "Chit Chat" is content-related, have learners add two or three ideas to their "Top Takeaways" page or notes section.
- If "Chit Chat" is brainstorming, pick a couple of ideas and add content in the moment.

# PRODUCER PROCESS

- Save the text chat at the end of the presentation.
- Assist learners with technical difficulties or questions.
- Put up timer for 2 minutes (variation only).

# VARIATIONS

- Have learners private text chat one other person to share ideas.
- In a time crunch, put up a timer for 2 minutes and have learners text chat on as many ideas as possible.
- Be specific about the content on which the learners should text chat.

**WEBINAR LENGTH:** Any

**ACTIVITY LENGTH:** 5 minutes

**INSTRUCTOR SKILL LEVEL:** Novice

**PARTICIPANT SKILL LEVEL:** Novice

**SUPPLIES:** Slide

**TOOLS:** Group Whiteboard

CLOSER
LEARNING ACTIVITY
**OPENER**
**SOFT OPENER**
**ENERGIZER**
REVISITER

# DOUBLE TROUBLE!

**PURPOSE:** Establish a Learning Community, Introduce New Concept, Refocus Learner

## SET-UP

- Create a slide that includes the following (these can be split into individual slides):
    - Title: Double Trouble
    - Feel, mood and kiss are words with double letters. Use the clues and fill in the blanks on the whiteboard and reveal the consecutive double letters. The words below have two sets of double letters!
    - Best part of waking up – c_ _ _ _ e
    - Foolish man – b_ _ _ _ _ n
    - Body graffiti – t_ _ _ _ o
    - Masked mammal – r_ _ _ _ _ n
    - Describing a sheep – w _ _ _ _ y
    - EXPERTS ONLY- try for this triple consecutive word
    - Systematic money recorder – b_ _ _ _ _ _ _ _ r
- Create a second slide that includes the answers:
    - Coffee
    - Buffoon
    - Tattoo
    - Raccoon
    - Woolly
    - Bookkeeper

**80**

- Insert the slide into the beginning of the presentation. Put up the slide prior to the webinar to help acclimate learners to the tools and to use as a soft opener. Insert at the beginning of the webinar if it is being used as an opener or anywhere throughout to be used as an energizer.

# TRAINER PROCESS

- Put up the "Double Trouble" slide.
- Ask learners to place their guesses or ideas on the whiteboard.
- When someone has the right answer, move on to the next slide.
- When that has been solved, ask participants to make a connection between the double consecutive letters and what is being learned or will be learned.
  - o Look for: sometimes we need to repeat ourselves, check and double check to make sure we've done the process correctly.
- No matter the riddle, it can be used as a quick way to energize a group and get brain cells firing again.

# PRODUCER PROCESS

- Welcome participants as they enter the virtual room via text chat.

# VARIATIONS

- Each learner is responsible for coming up with a word that has double letters. Post as many as possible in 90 seconds. Do the same for words with two and three sets of double letters. How does this relate to the content?
  - o Look For: collaboration increases production; teamwork; the more consecutive letters you have, the harder it becomes to solve can be compared to the complexity of a process with more steps.
- Use easier words for quicker reaction and response. For more advanced critical thinkers, use slightly more complex words.
- Tie the word puzzle to the content whenever possible. Use the word puzzle to transition to a new topic.

**WEBINAR LENGTH:** Any

**ACTIVITY LENGTH:** 5-10 minutes

**INSTRUCTOR SKILL LEVEL:** Novice

**PARTICIPANT SKILL LEVEL:** Novice

**SUPPLIES:** Slide

**TOOLS:** Group Text Chat, Group Whiteboard

**CLOSER**
**LEARNING ACTIVITY**
OPENER
SOFT OPENER
ENERGIZER
REVISITER

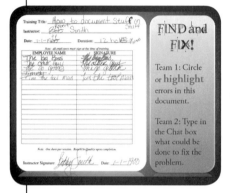

# FIND AND FIX

**PURPOSE:** Apply Material, Brainstorm, Combining, Familiarizing, Introduce New Concept, Recall Background Knowledge, Recall Information-Existing Schemas, Review

## SET-UP

- Create a "Find and Fix" slide that includes the following:
    - o A scanned-in form or document that has been incorrectly filled out. Examples of forms might be Good Manufacturing Practices (GMPs) or Standard Operating Procedures (SOPs).
    - o A small text box with these directions
        - Group 1-Highlight the errors
        - Group 2-Text Chat how the error can be fixed
- Insert the slide at the very beginning of the presentation as an opener, during a content piece to teach as a learning activity, after content is covered to revisit or as the last slide before break or the end of the session to be used as a closer.

# TRAINER PROCESS

- Put up the "Find and Fix" slide.
- Split group into two teams identified as Group 1 and Group 2.
  - Group 1-Highlight the errors
  - Group 2-Text Chat how the error can be fixed
- Demonstrate one error being highlighted and fixed via the text chat.
- As errors are found, read off what was found and affirm or deny the error.
- If being used as a learning activity, pause the group at various points and talk about each of the errors and make improvements or additions to the thoughts posted.
- If Group 2 is struggling with how the error can be fixed, pause the groups and discuss options.

# PRODUCER PROCESS

- During the demonstration, play the role of Group 2 and text chat how the error is fixed with the facilitator.
- Remove incorrect highlights.
- Put up timer (variation only).

# VARIATIONS

- Time the "Find and Fix" and see how many errors can be found in the countdown against the clock!
- For large groups, put learners into breakout rooms in groups of four. Two participants work on the errors and two work on the resolution.
- Turn it into a group relay race where any learner can either highlight an error or correct an error that has been highlighted.

**WEBINAR LENGTH:** Any

**ACTIVITY LENGTH:** 5 minutes

**INSTRUCTOR SKILL LEVEL:** Novice

**PARTICIPANT SKILL LEVEL:** Novice

**SUPPLIES:** Slide

**TOOLS:** Two-way Audio, Group Whiteboard

CLOSER
LEARNING ACTIVITY
OPENER
SOFT OPENER
ENERGIZER
REVISITER

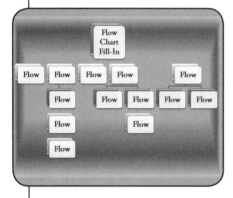

# FLOW CHART FILL-IN

**PURPOSE:** Combining, Familiarizing, Preview Material, Recall Background Knowledge, Recall Information-Existing Schemas, Refocus Learner, Review, Teach New Material

## SET-UP

- Create a "Flow Chart" slide that includes the following:
  - o Image of a flow chart that includes the steps to a process that participants are learning about or have prior knowledge about.
  - o Leave portions of the flow chart blank; participants will fill these in. The more the participants know about a process, the more blanks there should be. The more blanks, the more difficult.
- Insert the slide at the beginning of the session as an opener or at the end of the session as a closer. This slide can be used multiple times during a session. Fill it in as you go through each of the steps and enter the next phase of the flow chart.

## TRAINER PROCESS

- Put up the "Flow Chart" slide.
- Allow 90 seconds for learners to fill in the blanks in the flow chart as a group.

- Areas that learners do not fill in help to identify gaps in their learning.
- Share with learners that all areas of the process will be covered, but more time will be spent covering topic areas that are weaker for the group.
- If this is being done as a closer, learners should fill in the blanks and then whiteboard one takeaway from the piece of the flow chart they filled in.
- If you are using this as a closer after content is learned, insert a blank flow chart and have the group rotate filling in blanks and sharing learnings from each step of the process.

# PRODUCER PROCESS

- Put up timer for 90 seconds.

# VARIATIONS

- For large groups, do this in breakout rooms or select a smaller section of the group to write on the whiteboard.
- Insert the flow chart all throughout the session as a road map and insert as the group transitions from one portion of the flow chart to the next.
- Create a mind-map of content with blanks and have learners fill in the missing content pieces.
- If learners are new to the flow chart, add the flow chart topics on the page as a list and have learners work together and guess where they go in the process.

**WEBINAR LENGTH:** Any

**ACTIVITY LENGTH:** 1-5 minutes

**INSTRUCTOR SKILL LEVEL:** Novice

**PARTICIPANT SKILL LEVEL:** Novice

**SUPPLIES:** Slide

**TOOLS:** Polling

CLOSER
**LEARNING ACTIVITY**
OPENER
SOFT OPENER
**ENERGIZER**
**REVISITER**

# FROZEN ACRONYMS

**PURPOSE:** Familiarizing, Introduce New Concept, Recall Background Knowledge, Recall Information-Existing Schemas, Refocus Learner, Review, Teach New Material

## SET-UP

- Create a slide that includes the following:
  - o Title: Frozen Acronyms
  - o Do selected motion in place for 30 seconds or until the facilitator calls out a new acronym. Freeze when you hear an acronym.
  - o Raise your online hand if you know what the acronym stands for.
- Create a slide that includes a list of activities:
  - o Jumping
  - o Jumping jacks
  - o Stretching
  - o Twisting
  - o Playing air guitar
  - o Free choice
- Insert the slide at the very beginning of the presentation as an opener, during a content piece to teach as a learning activity, after content is covered to revisit or as the last slide before break or the end of the session to be used as a closer. Insert the slide anywhere throughout the presentation for fun as an energizer.

# TRAINER PROCESS

- Put up the "Frozen Acronym" direction slide when learners are starting to fade.
- Have learners stand at their desks. Encourage participation by demonstrating the movements on a webcam.
- Put up the activity slide and have participants select an activity from the list.
- Participants should do the activity for 30 seconds or until the facilitator calls out an acronym at which point participants freeze.
- Remind the group to raise their hand if they know the definition.
- Facilitator calls on a volunteer to either define the acronym or use it in a sentence.
- Tell learners to resume their activity or begin a new activity when their peer has defined the acronym.
- After all listed ideas are done, ask participants to text chat how they are feeling now compared to before they took their break.

# PRODUCER PROCESS

- Put on webcam and participate.
- Put up timer for 30 seconds. Reset and restart timer after each acronym.
- Post up ideas on whiteboard to get learners thinking (variation only).
- Keep track of team points (variation only).

# VARIATIONS

- Have learners stand and text chat the definition or sentence. The first correct text chat gets a point for their team. Make teams fun—guys vs. gals, East Coast vs. West Coast, etc. Use multiple times with the second half of the session earning double points.
- In need of a quick, unplanned energizer? Put up a blank whiteboard and have learners post, one at a time, acronyms along with an exercise. Learners still define the acronym.
- Do as a timed activity; get through as many acronyms as possible in the allotted time. Keep track of how many you get through each time to see if the number defined improves.

**WEBINAR LENGTH:** Any

**ACTIVITY LENGTH:** Varies

**INSTRUCTOR SKILL LEVEL:** Novice

**PARTICIPANT SKILL LEVEL:** Novice

**SUPPLIES:** Slide

**TOOLS:** Whiteboard

CLOSER

**LEARNING ACTIVITY**
**OPENER**

SOFT OPENER

**ENERGIZER**
**REVISITER**

# FULFILLING FILL-IN-THE BLANKS

**PURPOSE:** Apply Material, Brainstorm, Combining, Establish a Learning Community, Familiarizing, Innovate New Ideas, Introduce New Concept, Preview Material, Recall Background Knowledge, Recall Information-Existing Schemas, Refocus Learner, Review, Teach New Material

## SET-UP

- Create learner handouts that have blanks in several places during a piece of content.
- Create slides that include the answers to the blanks in their handouts. The fill-in-the-blank word should be highlighted and underlined.
    - o A sample slide could read:
        - Make **bullet points** visual.
- Insert the slide wherever the content falls initially, at the start of the second day of a webinar if it is to be used as a revisiting opener, or partway through the webinar if used as a revisiter.

# TRAINER PROCESS

- Have learners join you in their workbooks on the correct page.
- Begin lecturette and have learners fill in the blanks as the slides move along.
- Half-way through, have learners start or highlight in their workbooks the points that are most valuable to them.
- Continue through the slides until the section is complete.

# PRODUCER PROCESS

- Text chat the correct words as they come up.

# VARIATIONS

- If using two-way audio, have participants share their biggest takeaways from that section.
- Like competition? Have the fill-in answers at the bottom of the page and have learners guess what words fill in the blanks. Put up a timer for 90 seconds and see how many they can get.
- Put fill-in words on a slide and have learners share out loud what goes where. As they get one, share more about that piece of content or concept.

**WEBINAR LENGTH:** > 60 minutes, multi-day

**ACTIVITY LENGTH:** 5-10 minutes

**INSTRUCTOR SKILL LEVEL:** Novice

**PARTICIPANT SKILL LEVEL:** Novice

**SUPPLIES:** Slide

**TOOLS:** Group Text Chat

CLOSER
LEARNING ACTIVITY
OPENER
SOFT OPENER
ENERGIZER
REVISITER

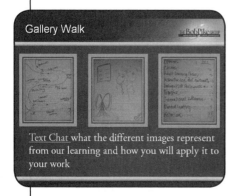

# GALLERY GUESSING
## GALLERY RECOGNITION

**PURPOSE:** Apply Material, Combining, Familiarizing, Introduce New Concept, Preview Material, Recall Background Knowledge, Recall Information-Existing Schemas, Refocus Learner, Review

## SET-UP

- Create a "Gallery Recognition" slide that includes images that represent concepts or ideas in the session (it could be a symbol or number that also represents important data to the topic).
- Insert the slide into the presentation at the beginning of the day as a soft opener (see variation), start of the second day of a webinar to be used as a revisiting opener, partway through the webinar if used as a revisiter for that day's content or, if used as a closer, before a break or at the very end of the session.

## TRAINER PROCESS

- Put up the "Gallery Recognition" slide.
- Have learners text chat the name of an image and what it represents from content learned or how it might relate to the topics of the day. Each learner will take a turn and rotate on to the next.

- Demonstrate to the class by text chatting an example. For example, if you have an image of "$," text the following: Dollar signs=increase revenue 2x in next 5 months or reduce spending by recycling.
- After text chatting an idea, the image can be highlighted or circled on the whiteboard. In smaller groups, this ensures all areas have been revisited.
- After all items are highlighted or circled, stop participants and instruct them to read back through the text chatting and what others have written.
- If used as a closer, have learners write down ideas on the "Top Takeaways" page or notes section.

## PRODUCER PROCESS

- Put up a timer for 1-3 minutes and have it count down (variation only).
- Save the text chat at the end of the presentation.

## VARIATIONS

- In small groups, assign an image to each participant.
- In larger groups, refrain from highlighting and circling assuming that with all of the learners each one will be touched on.
- In a time crunch, put up a timer for 2 minutes and have learners text chat on as many ideas as possible.
- In "Gallery Guessing," the learners only have an idea of course content and must try to make sense and meaning of the images. This could be used as a soft opener to begin generating ideas about what is to come. In this situation, there may be more than one correct interpretation.

**WEBINAR LENGTH:** Any

**ACTIVITY LENGTH:** 5-10 minutes

**INSTRUCTOR SKILL LEVEL:** Novice

**PARTICIPANT SKILL LEVEL:** Novice

**SUPPLIES:** Slide

**TOOLS:** Breakout Rooms, Group Whiteboard, Two-way Audio

CLOSER
**LEARNING ACTIVITY**
OPENER
SOFT OPENER
ENERGIZER
REVISITER

# GROUP WORK

**PURPOSE:** Apply Material, Brainstorm, Combining, Establish a Learning Community, Familiarizing, Innovate New Ideas, Recall Background Knowledge, Recall Information-Existing Schemas, Review, Teach New Material

## SET-UP

- Create a list of participants who will be in a group together. This can also be identified in the moment if participant numbers are unclear.
- Create a slide that includes the following:
  - o Title: "Creative Crew" or "Tactical Tribe"
  - o Share the following with each other:
    - Who you are
    - One tip you have for (insert content being covered)
    - What you are looking forward to during this session
  - o Team moderator is the person with the longest first name.
- Insert the slides wherever this content falls in the presentation.

## TRAINER PROCESS

- Split learners into groups of two to four people in each breakout room.

- Share that they will be going into breakout rooms in a moment. The tools are the same as in the main room and they will see the same slide as a reminder of what to do.
- Groups will have 5 minutes to answer the questions.
- Have groups "discuss" and, using the webinar platform tools (different colors, drawing tools, text, etc.), write these on their whiteboards.
- After the time is up, everyone will be back in the main room. Let these groups know they will be connecting with their "crew" throughout the session.
- Share how learners can get your attention for questions while in their rooms.
- Once learners are in their breakouts, move from room to room clarifying as needed.
- Have all groups come back together and have the team's moderators share what their group is looking forward to.

## PRODUCER PROCESS

- Create breakout rooms.
- Post pre-made slide in each breakout room with instructions.
- Put up a timer for 5 minutes and have it count down.
- Answer any questions that come through via text chat.
- Check in on breakout rooms and answer any questions.
- After time is up, post breakout room whiteboards in the main room for viewing or application share the whiteboards.

## VARIATIONS

- With small groups, do this in the main room as a single large group.
- Use this group or crew to brainstorm any topic or idea. Continually break back into the same group to problem solve or generate ideas on how to adapt, adopt or apply the material being taught.
- If first-time learners have not been in a breakout room before, don't have participants worry about tools–just have them share their ideas out loud.

**WEBINAR LENGTH:** Any

**ACTIVITY LENGTH:** 1-5 minutes

**INSTRUCTOR SKILL LEVEL:** Novice

**PARTICIPANT SKILL LEVEL:** Novice

**SUPPLIES:** Slide

**TOOLS:** Polling

CLOSER
LEARNING ACTIVITY
OPENER
SOFT OPENER
**ENERGIZER**
REVISITER

# HEART SMART

**PURPOSE:** Establishing a Learning Community, Refocus Learner

## SET-UP
- Create a slide that includes the following:
  - o Title: Heart Smart
  - o Raise your online hand and stand up if the listed idea is healthy.
  - o Put down your online hand if the listed idea is unhealthy.
- Create slide(s) that include the following ideas (do not include the sit/stand after the statement on the slide; they are for facilitator reference only). List of possible ideas:
  - o Riding a bike – stand
  - o Eating four pepperoni pizzas – sit
  - o Walking your dog – stand
  - o Smoking cigarettes – sit
  - o Dancing with your friends – stand
  - o Skating – stand
  - o Playing PlayStation – sit
  - o Eating fast food – sit
  - o Taking the stairs – stand
  - o Taking the elevator – sit
- Insert the slide anywhere throughout the presentation for fun as an energizer.

## TRAINER PROCESS

- Put up the "Heart Smart" direction slide when learners are starting to fade.
- Review the instructions on the slide.
  - o Raise your online hand and stand up if the listed idea is healthy.
  - o Put down your online hand if the listed idea is unhealthy.
- Share that a slide will be posted with a habit that strengthens or weakens the heart.
- If the habit strengthens the heart, participants should respond by standing up and raising their online hand. Demonstrate by raising your hand.
- If the habit weakens the heart, participants should respond by sitting down in their chair and lowering or keeping their hand down.
- Encourage participation by demonstrating the movements on a webcam.
- After all listed ideas are done, ask participants to text chat how they are feeling now compared to before they took their heart smart break.

## PRODUCER PROCESS

- Put on your webcam and participate.
- Post ideas on whiteboard to get learners thinking (variation only).
- Put up timer for 30-45 seconds (variation only).

## VARIATIONS

- Have learners stand and text chat when they did the last "Heart Smart" ideas.
- In need of a quick unplanned energizer? Put up a blank white board and have learners post, one at a time, healthy and unhealthy ideas. It is quick and easy to throw in at any time.
- Do as a timed activity and get through as many as possible in the allotted time.
- Have participants text chat, instead of whiteboard, habits they can think of.

**WEBINAR LENGTH:** Any

**ACTIVITY LENGTH:** 20-30 minutes

**INSTRUCTOR SKILL LEVEL:** Intermediate

**PARTICIPANT SKILL LEVEL:** Intermediate

**SUPPLIES:** Slide

**TOOLS:** Breakout Rooms, Group Whiteboard, Two-way Audio

CLOSER
**LEARNING ACTIVITY**
OPENER
SOFT OPENER
ENERGIZER
REVISITER

I OBJECT!

INSERT OBJECTION #1
INSERT OBJECTION #2
INSERT OBJECTION #3
INSERT OBJECTION #4

TEAM LEADER: PERSON WITH
THE LEAST YEARS WITH THE
ORGANIZATION.

# I OBJECT

**PURPOSE:** Apply Material, Brainstorm, Combining, Establish a Learning Community, Familiarizing, Innovate New Ideas, Recall Background Knowledge, Recall Information-Existing Schemas, Review, Teach New Material

## SET-UP

- Create a list of participants who will be in a group together. This can also be identified in the moment if participant numbers are unclear.
- Create a slide that includes the following:
  - o Title: I Object!
  - o Three to four different objections you have heard about the content, product, skill, and the list goes on.
  - o Team moderator is the person with the least number of years with the organization.
- Create a separate slide for each of the objections to be placed in breakout rooms with the "I Object" instructions slide.
- Insert the slides wherever this content falls in the presentation.

## TRAINER PROCESS

- Split learners into groups of two to four people in each breakout room.

- Each group is given a turn to select an objection from the list to work on in their breakout room.
- Each objection can be selected only once.
- Groups will have 3-7 minutes (depending on knowledge level and time needed to come up with valid points) to use prior knowledge as well as learning from the session to overcome their objection.
- Have groups "discuss" and, using the webinar platform tools (different colors, drawing tools, text, etc.), write these on their whiteboards.
- For example, participants can respond to an objection by stating a fact or feature about the product, and relating it, as a benefit, to the client's known needs.
- After the time is up, everyone will be back in the main room to share their objection and how they overcame it.
- Share how learners can get your attention for questions while in their rooms.
- Once learners are in their breakout rooms, move from room to room clarifying as needed.
- Have all groups come back together. The team's moderators will share their whiteboard with the group. Any ideas that are duplicated do not need to be covered again.

## PRODUCER PROCESS

- Create breakout rooms.
- Post pre-made slide with an objection in each breakout room with instructions.
- Put up a timer for 3-7 minutes and have it count down.
- Answer any questions that come through via text chat.
- Check in on breakout rooms and answer any questions.
- After time is up, post breakout room whiteboards in the main room for viewing or application share the whiteboards.

## VARIATIONS

- With small groups, do this in the main room together.
- Have breakout rooms groups come up with their own objection that another group will try to overcome.

97

**WEBINAR LENGTH:** Any

**ACTIVITY LENGTH:** 5-10 minutes

**INSTRUCTOR SKILL LEVEL:** Novice

**PARTICIPANT SKILL LEVEL:** Novice

**SUPPLIES:** Slide

**TOOLS:** Group Whiteboard

**CLOSER**
**LEARNING ACTIVITY**
**OPENER**
SOFT OPENER
ENERGIZER
**REVISITER**

# IDENTIFICATION SHUFFLE

**PURPOSE:** Familiarizing, Introduce New Concept, Preview Material, Recall Background Knowledge, Recall Information-Existing Schemas, Review, Teach New Material

## SET-UP

- Create an "Identification Shuffle" slide that includes the following:
  - o Investigative image inserted as a background
  - o Place eight to 10 correct process steps or concepts in a theory and eight to 10 incorrect process steps or concepts in a theory. Have them mixed together.
- Insert the slide into the presentation in the beginning as an opener, partway through the webinar if used as a revisiter or, if used as a closer, before a break or at the very end of the session. This can also be used at any point to transition content to a new topic or as a learning activity to solidify steps in a process.
- Create a handout page that lists all the steps in the correct sequence.

# TRAINER PROCESS

- Have learners close their workbooks for the next activity.
- Put up the "Identification Shuffle" slide.
- Have learners highlight an item in red that is not part of the process or highlight in green an item that is part of the process. Learners will take turns highlighting one item.
- If a participant doesn't know, they can then opt to type a number next to one of the items already highlighted to identify what step is first, second, third and so on in the process. If introducing a new topic, guessing is to be expected.
- Rotate around the group until all items are highlighted and numbered in the correct order.
- After each item is either removed or moved into sequence, talk about why it fits there and its importance to the process.
- After all items are done, discuss which items were correctly or incorrectly moved and spend some time on the errors and how to recall important steps or concepts.
- Refer learners to the page in their workbooks that has the items in the correct sequence.

# PRODUCER PROCESS

- Put up a timer for 1-3 minutes and have it count down or up (variation only).

# VARIATIONS

- If the platform being used allows for animation, insert hyperlinks that move the elements to a correct or incorrect side of the page so all participants have to do is click on the item.
- If your platform allows, click and drag the item to the correct side of the slide or to arrange it in the right sequence. Remove the item if it is not part of the sequence.
- To add to the fun, put on a timer or stopwatch to see how long it takes. You can also use a countdown timer and see how far they have gotten when time is up. The pieces that are out of order can then be discussed further.

**WEBINAR LENGTH:** Any

**ACTIVITY LENGTH:** 5-10 minutes

**INSTRUCTOR SKILL LEVEL:** Intermediate

**PARTICIPANT SKILL LEVEL:** Intermediate

**SUPPLIES:** Pre-made Interactive Game, Hyperlink to Activity

**TOOLS:** Group Text Chat, Polling

CLOSER
**LEARNING ACTIVITY**
OPENER
**SOFT OPENER**
**ENERGIZER**
REVISITER

# INTERACTIVE CROSSWORD PUZZLE

**PURPOSE:** Familiarizing, Introduce New Concept, Preview Material, Recall Background Knowledge, Refocus Learner, Review

## SET-UP

- Create a list of words that learners should become aware of or know by the end of a session. For each word, create a clue.
- Ensure whatever crossword product is selected can be played online. There are many freeware products out there that can be used to create an interactive crossword, but one I recommend for Microsoft users is found at EclipseCrossword.com. Eclipse Crossword is a fast, easy and free way to create crossword puzzles. There are several different printing options. For interaction, the site can save your crossword as a web page that won't require new software for users to download.
- Go through the tutorial if you want to be guided through the process.
- Once created, copy and paste the link into the leader's guide for quick reference.
- Take a screenshot of the game. Use this as your "Interactive Crossword Puzzle" slide and insert it into the slide deck at the appropriate point.
- Create a "Word List" slide with a list of all the words used in the crossword puzzle.

- Insert both slides, one after the other, in the beginning of the presentation if used as an opener for term recognition, at the end as the closer to reinforce concepts, or anywhere throughout to be used as an energizer, revisiter or learning activity.

# TRAINER PROCESS

- Put up the "Interactive Crossword" slide.
- Share with learners that they will have 3 minutes (or longer or shorter depending on the length of word search) to complete the crossword.
- Have learners click on the hyperlink in the text chat area (or copy and paste the link into a web browser if clicking doesn't work) and proceed to find the words.
- Put up the "Word List" slide.
- After the timer runs out, ask learners to raise their hand or select an emoticon to show that they are back in the room.
- See how learners did and where they struggled.
- Briefly go through and see what terms participants are unfamiliar with and provide explanations.

# PRODUCER PROCESS

- Make sure the link is working just before the session begins.
- Type the link into the text chat area for learners.
- Watch the text chat area for any questions.

# VARIATIONS

- Application share a web browser, and show learners what the crossword puzzle looks like while explaining how to do it. Model selecting a link.
- Give the link out in a welcome letter as a pre-session assignment.
- Use as a follow-up exercise for learners to recall information after the class.
- Save the crossword as a PDF or use the print options for inside the learner workbook.

**WEBINAR LENGTH:** Any

**ACTIVITY LENGTH:** 5-10 minutes

**INSTRUCTOR SKILL LEVEL:** Intermediate

**PARTICIPANT SKILL LEVEL:** Intermediate

**SUPPLIES:** Pre-made Interactive Game, Hyperlink to Activity

**TOOLS:** Group Text Chat, Polling

CLOSER
LEARNING ACTIVITY
OPENER
**SOFT OPENER**
ENERGIZER
REVISITER

# INTERACTIVE WORD SEARCH

**PURPOSE:** Familiarizing, Introduce New Concept, Preview Material, Recall Background Knowledge, Refocus Learner, Review

## SET-UP

- Create a word search, a grid of letters learners search through to find "hidden terms" associated with session content. Determine how hard you want to make the puzzle. The more ways a word can be found–vertically, horizontally, diagonally, backward and forward–the more difficult the puzzle.
- Ensure the word search product you use can be played online. One free online tool that can be used so all your learners can digitally "play" can be found on the Teacher's Direct website at http://bit.ly/wordfind. URL is case sensitive.
  - o Title the word search, then select any subject, then choose the size and type of search you wish to create. Select "15x15" for grid size, "interactive word search" for the word search type, and "lower case" for the text case. Then input the terms. Once completed, paste the link provided in your webinar so that learners can paste it in their browsers and quickly get to the word search.
- Take a screenshot of the game and use as your "Interactive Word Search" slide. Insert into the slide deck early in your

presentation to help learners recognize terms, or place it later to reinforce terminology.

- Create a "Word List" slide with a list of all the words used in the word search.
- Insert both slides together at the beginning of the presentation if used as an opener, at the end as the closer or anywhere throughout to be used as an energizer, revisiter or learning activity.

# TRAINER PROCESS

- Put up the "Interactive Word Search" slide.
- Share with learners that they will have 3 minutes (longer or shorter depending on length of word search) to complete the word search.
- As they find words they are unfamiliar with, they should jot them down to explore once they are back in the webinar.
- Have learners click on the hyperlink in the text chat area (or copy and paste the link into a web browser) and find the words.
- Put up the "Word List" slide.
- After the timer runs out, ask learners to raise their hand or select an emoticon to show that they are back in the room.
- Briefly go through and see what terms participants are unfamiliar with and provide an explanation.

# PRODUCER PROCESS

- Make sure the link is working just before the session begins.
- Type the link into the text chat area for learners.
- Watch the text chat area for any questions.

# VARIATIONS

- Application share a web browser and show learners what the interactive word search looks like while explaining how to do it. Model selecting a link.
- Give the link in a welcome letter as a pre-session assignment.
- Use as a follow-up exercise for learners to recall information after the class.
- Save the word search as a PDF or print it for inside the learner workbook.

**WEBINAR LENGTH:** Any

**ACTIVITY LENGTH:** 5 minutes

**INSTRUCTOR SKILL LEVEL:** Novice

**PARTICIPANT SKILL LEVEL:** Novice

**SUPPLIES:** Slide

**TOOLS:** Group Whiteboard

CLOSER
LEARNING ACTIVITY
OPENER
SOFT OPENER
ENERGIZER
REVISITER

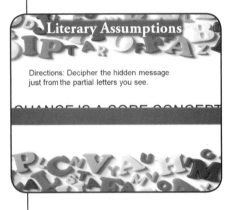

# LITERARY ASSUMPTIONS

**PURPOSE:** Brainstorm, Establish a Learning Community, Familiarizing, Introduce New Concept, Recall Background Knowledge, Recall Information-Existing Schemas, Refocus Learner, Teach New Material

## SET-UP

- Create a slide that includes the following (these can be split into individual slides):
  - o Title: Literary Assumptions
  - o ~~CHANGE IS A CORE CONCEPT~~
  - o ~~CHUNK CONCEPTS INTO SMALL PARTS~~
  - o Directions: Decipher the hidden message just from the partial letters you see.
- Create a second slide that includes the answer. Samples:
  - o CHANGE IS A CORE CONCEPT
  - o CHUNK CONTENT INTO SMALL PARTS
- Insert the slide into the beginning of the presentation. Put up the slide prior to the webinar as a soft opener to help acclimate learners to the platform tools. If this is to be used as an opener, insert the slide at the start of the session. To use this as an energizer, insert the slide anywhere.

# TRAINER PROCESS

- Put up the "Literary Assumptions" slide.
- Ask learners to decipher the hidden message just from the partial letters they see and whiteboard their guesses.
- After 90 seconds, continue to the next content piece if this is used as an energizer. If this is used as an opener, ask participants to whiteboard what insights can be taken away from this exercise.
    - o Look for: sometimes when doing things too quickly, assumptions are made from past experience; when we are experts, we take what we know for granted; common knowledge can get in the way of seeing things clearly.

# PRODUCER PROCESS

- Welcome participants as they enter the virtual room via text chat.
- Whiteboard an idea or two to spur thoughts.
- Turn on the timer for 30-60 seconds (variation only).

# VARIATIONS

- Create a phrase that directly relates to the content being taught.
- Have a dialogue with learners about assumptions via two-way audio. Call on participants one at a time.
- Have learners work individually at first to come up with words and then, after 30-60 seconds, have them work together. Debrief with questions like: What helped you to be successful? What does success look like? What insights can we take away from this exercise and apply back at work?
- Tie the puzzle to the content whenever possible.
- Use the puzzle to transition to a new topic.

**WEBINAR LENGTH:** Any

**ACTIVITY LENGTH:** 5 minutes

**INSTRUCTOR SKILL LEVEL:** Novice

**PARTICIPANT SKILL LEVEL:** Novice

**SUPPLIES:** Slide

**TOOLS:** Group Whiteboard, Group Text Chat

CLOSER
LEARNING ACTIVITY
**OPENER**
**SOFT OPENER**
**ENERGIZER**
REVISITER

Map It – Where are we?

# MAP IT

**PURPOSE:** Brainstorm, Establish a Learning Community

## SET-UP

- Create a slide that includes the following (these can be split into individual slides):
    o Title: Where Are We?
    o Large image of the United States (or world map or state map)
    o Directions: Using a pointer or highlighter, mark the spot where you are right now.
- Insert the slide into the beginning of the presentation. Put up the slide prior to the webinar as a soft opener to help acclimate learners to the platform tools. If this is to be used as an opener, insert the slide at the start of the session. To use this as an energizer, insert the slide anywhere.

## TRAINER PROCESS

- Put up the "Where Are We?" slide.
- Ask learners to use their tools and point or highlight the spot where they are located. Then have learners text chat the exact location and what the weather is like.

**106**

- Model highlighting on the whiteboard and text chat what the weather is like.
- Act as an announcer and read off where people are from.

# PRODUCER PROCESS

- Welcome participants as they enter the virtual room via text chat.
- Highlight on whiteboard where you are at and text chat the weather there.

# VARIATIONS

- If using two-way audio, have participants, one at a time, share a little about their climate or what they are looking forward to.
- Ask learners questions or trivia about their state.
- After highlighting where they are, have learners highlight where they are dreaming of going or where they wish they were on the map. Text chat the exact location and why.

**WEBINAR LENGTH:** > 60 minutes

**ACTIVITY LENGTH:** 10-15 minutes

**INSTRUCTOR SKILL LEVEL:** Intermediate

**PARTICIPANT SKILL LEVEL:** Intermediate

**SUPPLIES:** Slide

**TOOLS:** Breakout Rooms, Group Whiteboard, Two-way Audio

CLOSER
LEARNING ACTIVITY
**OPENER**
SOFT OPENER
**ENERGIZER**
REVISITER

# MASTER-MIND MIX

**PURPOSE:** Brainstorm, Establish a Learning Community, Familiarizing, Introduce New Concept, Recall Background Knowledge, Recall Information-Existing Schemas, Refocus Learner

## SET-UP

- Determine the number of participants and what breakout rooms will be named.
- Create a slide that includes the following:
  - o Title: Mastermind Mix
  - o The image in the background should be of two minds meeting
  - o Each member introduce themselves
  - o Share one fact, concept or idea they already know about today's webinar or topic
- Insert the slide into the presentation in the beginning as an opener or anywhere throughout the session as an energizer.

## TRAINER PROCESS

- Put up the "Mastermind Mix" slide.
- Share that there are participants in this webinar that are going to really take their level of understanding with this topic to a new

level. There are several who already know something about the webinar topic–it could be a piece of data, terminology or something about using webinars.

- Have learners take a look at the list of names of those in the session.
- Share that it is an honor to be on this webinar with everyone and that they will find masters all throughout our list.
- Share that learners will be in breakout rooms in a moment. They will have 3 minutes to introduce themselves, and share one fact, concept or idea about the session topic they already know. This will then become their Mastermind group for the session. From time to time, they will have a "meeting of the minds" and be breaking out with them.
- Ask if there are questions about the directions.
- Split participants into breakout rooms with three to five participants in each.
- Send groups into their assigned breakout rooms for 3 minutes.
- Return teams to the main room.

## PRODUCER PROCESS

- Create breakout rooms.
- Post the "Mastermind Mix" slide in each breakout room.
- Send learners into their breakout rooms.
- Put up a timer for 3 minutes and have it count down.
- Check in on breakout rooms and answer any questions.

## VARIATIONS

- If you have a small group, stay in the main room together.
- Have learners create a whiteboard that represents their mastermind team and what they shared with each other.

**WEBINAR LENGTH:** > 90 minutes

**ACTIVITY LENGTH:** 6-13 minutes

**INSTRUCTOR SKILL LEVEL:** Novice

**PARTICIPANT SKILL LEVEL:** Novice

**SUPPLIES:** Slide

**TOOLS:** Whiteboard

CLOSER
LEARNING ACTIVITY
OPENER
SOFT OPENER
**ENERGIZER**
REVISITER

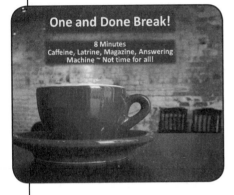

# ONE AND DONE BREAK
## (AKA THE ONE-FUNCTION BREAK)

**PURPOSE:** Refocus Learner

## SET-UP

- Determine the length of the break. The longer the webinar, the longer the break. Break times that work well:
    - o 2-hour session = 6- to 8-minute break at the 60-minute mark
    - o 2 ½-hour session = 9- to 10-minute break between 75-90 minutes
    - o 3-hour session = 11- to 15-minute break at the 90-minute mark OR two shorter breaks at the 1-and 2-hour marks. Depending on the content, it may be better to provide two 6-minute breaks to help with the flow of content. If concerned about participants not arriving back on time from shorter breaks, opt for one longer break.
- Create a slide and include the following:
    - o Title: One and Done Break
    - o The amount of time the break will be
- Insert the slide into the session at the 60-, 75- or 90-minute mark.

# TRAINER PROCESS

- Explain that the group will be taking a "One and Done" break in a moment.
- Put up the "One and Done" slide.
- Describe the break: You have time to smoke or make a phone call, use the restroom, check an email or text chat us a question, but not time for all.
- Don't fret about losing people. If your content is interactive and engaging, they'll be back.

# PRODUCER PROCESS

- Put up a timer and have it count down.
- Answer any questions that come through via text chat.
- Create breakout rooms and distribute participants (variation only).
- Check in on breakout rooms and help answer questions (variation only).

# VARIATIONS

- Create assignments for each person to accomplish while on break. This would be considered a "working break" where there is enough time to accomplish the task and still have time left over for a one and done break.
- Extend the break time and incorporate a small group discussion in breakout rooms with teach-back points they are responsible for sharing with the large group.

111

**WEBINAR LENGTH:** Any

**ACTIVITY LENGTH:** 2-5 minutes

**INSTRUCTOR SKILL LEVEL:** Novice

**PARTICIPANT SKILL LEVEL:** Novice

**SUPPLIES:** Slide

**TOOLS:** Polling, Two-way Audio

CLOSER
LEARNING ACTIVITY
OPENER
SOFT OPENER
**ENERGIZER**
**REVISITER**

# OOHHRAH CHEER

**PURPOSE:** Apply Material, Combining, Familiarizing, Recall Background Knowledge, Recall Information-Existing Schemas, Review

## SET-UP

- Create the session slide deck
- Within the deck, insert errors
    - o Errors could be anything from changing the name of a product, giving an incorrect data piece (later in the presentation) to spelling or grammatical errors.
    - o Errors later in the deck should be about content previously learned to be used as a revisit technique.
- Insert slides wherever they would fall in the content flow. Purposely insert errors throughout at good revisit points.

## TRAINER PROCESS

- At the beginning of the session, let learners know that errors have been "planted" on slides and that there are fabulous semi-valuable prizes for those that catch the errors.
- Whenever a participant catches an error, they may raise their virtual hand, be called on, turn on their microphone and cheer "OOHHRAH."

- They will then share what the error was and how it should be corrected.
- If learners miss a content error, pause and ask, "What is wrong with this slide?"
- Wait and see if they can figure it out.

# PRODUCER PROCESS

- Keep track of error slides and prompt the facilitator if one is missed.
- Keep track of learners that raise their hand and shout OOOHHRAH.
- Send out a prize to the winning participant.

# VARIATIONS

- At the end of the session, ask learners to whiteboard or chat about this question: "What does finding errors in this session have to do with our topic today?" Look for things that relate to the session. For example: stopping to correct errors right away saves time and money.
- Instead of shouting OOHHRAH, have learners highlight anything they find wrong as an error along the way.

**WEBINAR LENGTH:** Any

**ACTIVITY LENGTH:** 1-5 minutes

**INSTRUCTOR SKILL LEVEL:** Novice

**PARTICIPANT SKILL LEVEL:** Novice

**SUPPLIES:** Slide, UNO cards optional

**TOOLS:** Whiteboard

CLOSER
LEARNING ACTIVITY
OPENER
SOFT OPENER
**ENERGIZER**
REVISITER

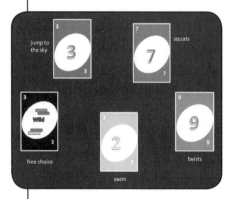

# PASS IT ON— UNO™ STYLE

**PURPOSE:** Establishing a Learning Community, Refocus Learner

## SET-UP

- Create an "UNO" slide that includes the following:
    - Images of UNO-style cards. At least one of each color card should be represented. Include a wild card.
- Create a second slide that includes the following:
    - Blue: jump to the sky
    - Red: squats
    - Yellow: twist
    - Green: swim
    - Wild: free choice
- Insert the slide anywhere in the deck for fun as an energizer.

## TRAINER PROCESS

- Put up the "UNO" slide when learners are starting to fade.
- Have a participant volunteer and select an UNO card from the screen and circle it.
- Once circled, share that this is the activity they get to do for 30 seconds to get the blood moving.
- If a wild card is selected, it is free choice for the activity.

- Turn on your webcam to demonstrate the 30-second activity.
- After the timer is done, ask participants to text chat how they are feeling now compared to before they took a "swim."

# PRODUCER PROCESS

- Put up the timer for 30 seconds.

# VARIATIONS

- Instead of 30 seconds, base it on the number selected. The number selected equals the number of times the activity is done. Example: If a Red 7 is selected, participants would do seven squats.
- Create a slide with enough UNO cards so that each person will have one. Each participant circles a card on the whiteboard and types their name above or below the card. After they have completed the activity associated with their card, they pass their card to another participant by drawing a line to another card.
- If using a webcam, hold up a deck of UNO cards and have a learner tell you when to stop. The card stopped on is the card selected. Continue with the same exercise rules.

**WEBINAR LENGTH:** Any

**ACTIVITY LENGTH:** 5 minutes

**INSTRUCTOR SKILL LEVEL:** Novice

**PARTICIPANT SKILL LEVEL:** Novice

**SUPPLIES:** Slide

**TOOLS:** Group Text Chat

CLOSER
LEARNING ACTIVITY
**OPENER**
**SOFT OPENER**
**ENERGIZER**
REVISITER

# PESKY PALINDROMES

**PURPOSE:** Establish a Learning Community, Introduce New Concept, Refocus Learner

## SET-UP

- Create a slide that includes the following (these can be split into individual slides):
    - o Title: Pesky Palindromes
    - o Image in the background of a lot of scattered letters.
    - o Whiteboard as many words as you can that read the same backward and forward that are 3, 4, 5, 6 or 7 letters long. Example: aha
- Create a second slide that includes some answers (optional):
    - o 3 letters–aha, bib, dad, did, hah, mom, bob, tot, wow
    - o 4 letters–noon, peep, poop, ma'am, sees, toot
    - o 5 letters–kayak, level, madam, stats, radar, refer, rotor, sexes
    - o 6 letters–redder, denned
    - o 7 Letters–racecar, repaper, reviver, rotator, deified, a Toyota
- Insert the slide into the beginning of the presentation. Put up the slide prior to the webinar as a soft opener to help acclimate learners to the platform tools. If this is to be used as an opener,

insert the slide at the start of the session. To use this as an energizer, insert the slide anywhere.

## TRAINER PROCESS

- Put up the "Pesky Palindromes" slide.
- Ask learners to text chat their ideas for 60 seconds.
- After time is up, move on to the next slide.
- Discuss connections between palindromes and what is being learned or will be learned. Have learners text chat their ideas. Read them out loud as they come up.
  - o Look for: look at information from multiple angles and make sure we get the same answer; the longer the process, the more difficult to ensure it works both ways.
- No matter the length of the palindrome, the exercise can be used as a quick way to energize a group and get brain cells firing again.

## PRODUCER PROCESS

- Welcome participants as they enter the virtual room via text chat.

## VARIATIONS

- Create a list of just the first and last letter of the palindrome and see how many get filled in. Example: A_A, B_B, K_ _ _ K, R _ _ _ R and so on. Time it for 30 seconds for a quick energizer.
- Brainstorm only three-letter words for quicker reaction and response. For more advanced critical thinkers, limit responses to five-letters or longer.
- Tie the word puzzle to the content whenever possible. Use the word puzzle to transition to a new topic.

**WEBINAR LENGTH:** Any

**ACTIVITY LENGTH:** 1-5 minutes

**INSTRUCTOR SKILL LEVEL:** Novice

**PARTICIPANT SKILL LEVEL:** Novice

**SUPPLIES:** Slide

**TOOLS:** Polling

CLOSER
**LEARNING ACTIVITY**
OPENER
SOFT OPENER
ENERGIZER
**REVISITER**

# POP QUIZ
## (PUZZLE)

**PURPOSE:** Apply Material, Introduce New Concept, Preview Material, Recall Background Knowledge, Recall Information-Existing Schemas, Refocus Learner, Review, Teach New Material

## SET-UP

- Become familiar with polling options on the platform you will be using.
- Create pre-made "Pop Quiz" question slide(s) and include a small screenshot of where the polling icons are located.
- Write up to three questions on each slide that relate to content that was or will be covered during the session.
    o Number the question.
    o Create as many question slides as desired.
    o Create a Pop Quiz answer slide(s). Put all questions and their answers on the slide(s). Number each answer.
- Quiz questions on each slide should all be the same type: Yes/No, True/False, A-E etc.
- Insert the "Pop Quiz" slides as the first slide if used as an opener to get a pulse on where learners are at with the content. Insert throughout for revisiting or energizing and at the end as the last slide if closing out the session with a "Pop Quiz."
- Insert the "Pop Quiz" answer slide(s) after each "Pop Quiz" slide or after the final "Pop Quiz."

# TRAINER PROCESS

- Put up the first "Pop Quiz" slide.
- Explain that throughout the webinar there will be "Pop Quiz" slides.
- When these slides "pop up," each person will use their polling tools to answer the questions.
- After everyone has answered, show the learner results, and then the correct answer can be defined. If used as an opener, follow each slide up with teaching the content from the slide questions. If the platform doesn't allow for results to be shown, have learners keep track of their answers and correct themselves when the answer slide is revealed.

# PRODUCER PROCESS

- Prior to the questions going up on the whiteboard, be sure to change polling from a pacing feature to a yes/no feature or true/false question if the correct polling features are not standard on the platform.

# VARIATIONS

- The term "quiz" may have negative connotations. To make it more fun and light, use the word "puzzle" instead.
- If you need a quick engager and haven't had a chance to prepare a slide, add a whiteboard and insert a question in the moment.
- Have a competitive crowd? Grade the quizzes and have learners keep track of their own score. Award more points for harder questions. Add the point value to each slide.
- Pop quizzes do not need to be graded; however, they give the facilitator a pulse as to what may need reemphasizing.
- If the platform being used doesn't have polling options, create the questions and answers on a whiteboard and have participants highlight or mark the answer they think is correct.

**WEBINAR LENGTH:** Any

**ACTIVITY LENGTH:** 1-5 minutes

**INSTRUCTOR SKILL LEVEL:** Novice

**PARTICIPANT SKILL LEVEL:** Novice

**SUPPLIES:** Slide

**TOOLS:** Group Text Chat, Polling

CLOSER
**LEARNING ACTIVITY**
OPENER
SOFT OPENER
**ENERGIZER**
**REVISITER**

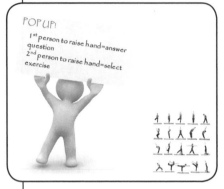

# POP UPS

**PURPOSE:** Apply Material, Introduce New Concept, Preview Material, Recall Background Knowledge, Recall Information-Existing Schemas, Refocus Learner, Review, Teach New Material

## SET-UP

- Create a "Pop Up" rules slide with the following rules:
    - o 1st person to raise hand=answer question
    - o 2nd person to raise hand=select exercise
    - o Everyone=pop up and do exercise while question is being answered [modify these rules as needed].
- Create pre-made question slide(s) and include a small screenshot of where the "raise hand" icon is located.
    - o Write one question on the slide about content covered.
    - o Across the bottom of the slide, list out five different types of exercises. Examples: Toe Touch, Twists, Jumping Jacks
    - o Create as many question slides as needed.
- Become familiar with signals on the platform you will be using.
- Insert the "Pop Up" rules slide toward the beginning of the presentation but after the webinar opener and session agenda.
- Insert the slide(s) into the presentation at any point as an energizer and revisit technique. Increase the number of "Pop Up" slides as presentations get longer.

# TRAINER PROCESS

- Put up the "Pop Up" rules slide.
- Explain that throughout the webinar there will be "Pop Up" slides that look like this. Put up an example of a "Pop Up" question slide.
- When these slides "pop up," the first person to raise their hand and share the answer receives a point.
- Points can accumulate during a single or multiple sessions. Pop ups can also be random facts about the company or product.
- The second person to raise their hand selects one of the exercises listed on the bottom of the "Pop Up" question slide. All other learners then "Pop Up" and do the exercise continuously while the first person answers the question.
- If the question is answered incorrectly, the question goes to the second person who raises their hand. If it is still answered incorrectly, the instructor reveals the answer to the group.
- Turn on your webcam to demonstrate standing up and then the model the selected exercise.

# PRODUCER PROCESS

- Before the questions go on the whiteboard, make sure the polling has the correct features (e.g., from pacing to yes/no) if the polling features are not standard on the platform.

# VARIATIONS

- If you need a quick engager and haven't had a chance to prepare a slide, just add a whiteboard and insert a question in the moment.
- Have a competitive crowd? Late in the day put up a timer for 2-5 minutes and have learners answer as many "Pop Up" questions as possible to earn last minute points.
- Double the pop up point worth in the last portion of the webinar.
- If a "raise hand" signal button isn't available on your platform, try using a different signal button. This could be a smiley face or learners could clap.
- Have learners accumulate points over multiple sessions.

**WEBINAR LENGTH:** Any

**ACTIVITY LENGTH:** 5-15 minutes

**INSTRUCTOR SKILL LEVEL:** Novice

**PARTICIPANT SKILL LEVEL:** Novice

**SUPPLIES:** Slide

**TOOLS:** Whiteboard and Drawing/Writing Tools – Optional Text Chat, Breakout Rooms

CLOSER
LEARNING ACTIVITY
OPENER
SOFT OPENER
ENERGIZER
REVISITER

# Q IT UP

**PURPOSE:** Brainstorm, Establish a Learning Community, Introduce New Concept, Recall Background Knowledge, Review

## SET-UP

- Create a handout titled "Questions" for learners to compile questions during the webinar.
- Create a slide that includes the following:
  - o  Title: Q It Up
  - o  Image of a large "?"
- Insert the slide into the presentation at the beginning of a second webinar as an opener, anywhere throughout to revisit or energize, before a break or at the very end of the session as a closing exercise.

## TRAINER PROCESS

- Have learners turn to their "Questions" page.
- Put up the "Q It Up" slide.
- Share that the group will have 60 seconds to review their questions and cross off questions that have been answered. Then they may post as many questions as they are able in the time allotted.

- When working with the same learners over the course of several webinars, there may be "parking lot" questions that need to be answered.
- Answer posted questions.
- If used as a closer, each participant can write a question on the whiteboard from content that was already covered. In some cases they may already know the answer; in others, they may have missed something and need the information. After questions are up, each participant text chats (or writes on the whiteboard) the answer to a question they did not write. These questions can then be used in a subsequent webinar as quiz questions or for another exercise.
- If used as a revisit or opener technique, have learners write their questions in the first webinar and have each question posted in the second webinar. Each group will take a question and have 2-4 minutes in their breakout rooms to come up with an answer. Alternately pre-select questions at random and post in their breakout rooms. Learners will write the answer to their question(s) on the whiteboard. Bring everyone back into the main room and go from one question to the next with their posted answers.

## PRODUCER PROCESS

- Put up a timer for 60 seconds.
- Answer/post any questions that come through via text chat.
- Copy whiteboard questions for future use.
- Put up a timer for 5 minutes (variation only).

## VARIATIONS

- Used pre-made content questions and have learners post their answers on the whiteboard. Or post the answer and have learners whiteboard the question.
- To ensure the question-and-answer session doesn't take too long, use a countdown timer and post 5 minutes.
- Have learners post only questions for which they do not have an answer.

**WEBINAR LENGTH:** Any

**ACTIVITY LENGTH:** 1-5 minutes

**INSTRUCTOR SKILL LEVEL:** Novice

**PARTICIPANT SKILL LEVEL:** Novice

**SUPPLIES:** Slide

**TOOLS:** Group Whiteboard

CLOSER
LEARNING ACTIVITY
OPENER
SOFT OPENER
ENERGIZER
**REVISITER**

# QUICK QUESTIONS

**PURPOSE:** Apply Material, Recall Background Knowledge, Refocus Learner, Review

## SET-UP

- Create a list of questions pertaining to the content and have it written down in the leader's guide.
- Create a list of acceptable answers to those questions.
- Create a slide(s) that has a list of all the questions and answers (Q&A).

## TRAINER PROCESS

- At any time in the session, insert a clean whiteboard slide and type a question to interject some variety and interest.
- Announce that learners will only have a set amount of time (30 seconds) to jot down their answer on note paper.
- Do this several times throughout the webinar.
- At the end of the session, take those same questions and have people share their answers at random.
- Thank the learners for sharing.
- Post the "Q&A" slide for all to see acceptable answers.

## PRODUCER PROCESS

- Put up a timer for 30 seconds.
- Capture learner questions (variation only).

## VARIATIONS

- Make it competitive and the person with the most correct answers wins a small prize.
- Have learners volunteer to post a question in the moment.

**WEBINAR LENGTH:** Any

**ACTIVITY LENGTH:** 5-20 minutes

**INSTRUCTOR SKILL LEVEL:** Intermediate

**PARTICIPANT SKILL LEVEL:** Novice

**SUPPLIES:** Slide

**TOOLS:** Application Share, Two-way Audio

CLOSER
**LEARNING ACTIVITY**
OPENER
**SOFT OPENER**
ENERGIZER
REVISITER

# RAPTIVITY™

**PURPOSE**: Apply Material, Brainstorm, Combining, Establish a Learning Community, Familiarizing, Innovate New Ideas, Introduce New Concept, Preview Material, Recall Background Knowledge, Recall Information-Existing Schemas, Refocus Learner, Review, Teach New Material

## SET-UP

- Purchase Raptivity software or download a free trial license at Raptivity.com.
- Select an interactive game that suits the content. More than 225 interactive options are available, ranging from videos to simulations to matching games. All are colorful and all can be housed online for learners to do on their own.
- Create and test the game.
- Create a slide that includes the following:
  - Directions on how the game works. This will vary based on the exercise selected by the facilitator.

# TRAINER PROCESS

- Launch the Raptivity game.
- Start the game and ask participants to raise their hand if they think they know the answer.
- Continue getting answers to game questions until the exercise is done.
- Stop application sharing and have participants text chat learnings from the exercise. Continue with a lecturette on the topics or content covered.

# PRODUCER PROCESS

- Monitor text chat and respond to questions.

# VARIATIONS

- For more experienced users, turn over control to a participant and have them click through the game and get answers from the group.
- Have learners go through the game on their own and then application share the game and talk through the different concepts and elements.
- Intersperse the game throughout the session and do a few questions or elements at a time.

**WEBINAR LENGTH:** Any

**ACTIVITY LENGTH:** Varies

**INSTRUCTOR SKILL LEVEL:** Intermediate

**PARTICIPANT SKILL LEVEL:** Novice

**SUPPLIES:** Slide, Web Address for Response Pads

**TOOLS:** Application Share, Two-way Audio, Responseware

CLOSER
LEARNING ACTIVITY
OPENER
SOFT OPENER
ENERGIZER
REVISITER

ⓣ ResponseWare

# RESPONSE-WARE™

**PURPOSE:** Apply Material, Brainstorm, Combining, Establish a Learning Community, Familiarizing, Innovate New Ideas, Introduce New Concept, Preview Material, Recall Background Knowledge, Recall Information-Existing Schemas, Refocus Learner, Review, Teach New Material

## SET-UP

- Purchase ResponseWare software by calling 1-866-746-3015 or download a free license for up to 5 responses at TurningTechnologies.com.
- Create question slides but don't overload the presentation with questions and choices.
- Types of Questions:
  - o Soft Opener–Ask an off-topic question so participants are familiar with how the keypads work. Provide clear instructions on how to respond.
  - o Learning Activity–Ask useful questions that are in alignment with your objectives. Ask learners to guess at answers and then share content.
  - o Survey Questions–These provide the facilitator with a lot of information and let other learners know they are not alone. A great way to open up dialogue.
- Create and test a question slide. Keep the content short.

- Insert www.rwpoll.com link and session code into leader's guide for quick reference.
- Create a "ResponseWare" slide that includes the following:
  - o Image of the rwpoll page and image of the response pad.
  - o Directions on how to use the polling. This will vary based on the exercise selected by the facilitator.
  - o Link to www.rwpoll.com.
- Insert question slides all throughout the webinar.

# TRAINER PROCESS

- Put up the "ResponseWare" slide.
- Launch ResponseWare on the facilitator desktop.
- Have learners click on the hyperlink. Let them know a new window will open which can be moved around so that they are still able to see the facilitator's screen and platform.
- Once the window pops up, enter the session code.
- Wait for learners while they do this.
- Start ResponseWare and ask the questions. Have participants ring in with their virtual pads. Continue getting answers to game questions until the questions are done.
- Stop application sharing and have learners text chat learnings from the exercise.

# PRODUCER PROCESS

- Help participants get up and running with the keypads.
- Monitor text chat area while polling is in play.

# VARIATIONS

- Try multiple choice, multiple response, priority ranking, matching and "true" or "false", fill-in-the-blank, short answer and essay questions.
- Have learners go through their own version.
- Have learners compete for fastest responder.
- Assign point values to questions.
- Include countdown timers to force an answer in a timely fashion and keep things moving.

**WEBINAR LENGTH:** Any

**ACTIVITY LENGTH:** 5 minutes

**INSTRUCTOR SKILL LEVEL:** Novice

**PARTICIPANT SKILL LEVEL:** Novice

**SUPPLIES:** Slide

**TOOLS:** Group Text Chat

CLOSER
LEARNING ACTIVITY
**OPENER**
**SOFT OPENER**
**ENERGIZER**
REVISITER

# REVERSIBLE REFLECTION

**PURPOSE:** Establish a Learning Community, Introduce New Concept, Refocus Learner

## SET-UP

- Create a slide that includes the following (these can be split into individual slides):
  - o Title: Reversible Reflection
  - o Image in the background of a lot of random words scattered around as a watermark.
- Directions: Text chat as many words as you can that are real words when read forward and backward. One example is Gateman/Nametag.
- Create a second slide that includes some answers (optional):
  - o Lived/devil, drawer/reward, desserts/stressed, diaper/repaid
- Insert the slide into the beginning of the presentation. Put up the slide prior to the webinar as a soft opener to help acclimate learners to the platform tools. If this is to be used as an opener, insert the slide at the start of the session. To use this as an energizer, insert the slide anywhere.

# TRAINER PROCESS

- Put up the "Reversible Reflection" slide.
- Ask learners to place their guesses or ideas on the whiteboard.
- After 90 seconds, continue on to the next content piece if this is used as an energizer. If used as an opener, ask participants to make a connection between reversible words and what is being learned or will be learned.
  - o Look for: discovering how words can be read both ways is like learning—learning is a discovery process; the content we are looking at is intentional just like we are looking for words that are intentional; humans have a need-to-know attitude and when searching for these words, we realize we really want to get the answer.

# PRODUCER PROCESS

- Welcome participants as they enter the virtual room via text chat.
- Whiteboard an idea or two to spur thoughts.

# VARIATIONS

- Create a list of just the first and last letter of the reversible word and see how many get filled in. Example: A_A, B_B, G_ _ _ _ _N, K_ _ _ K, D_ _ _ _ _ _ S and so on. Time it for 30-60 seconds for a quick energizer.
- Brainstorm only three-letter words for quicker reaction and response. For more advanced critical thinkers, limit responses to five letters or longer.
- Tie the word puzzle to the content whenever possible. Use the word puzzle to transition to a new topic.

**WEBINAR LENGTH:** Any

**ACTIVITY LENGTH:** 5 minutes

**INSTRUCTOR SKILL LEVEL:** Novice

**PARTICIPANT SKILL LEVEL:** Novice

**SUPPLIES:** Slide

**TOOLS:** Group Text Chat

CLOSER
LEARNING ACTIVITY
**OPENER**
**SOFT OPENER**
**ENERGIZER**
REVISITER

Riddle Me This

**Text Chat Your Guess**

Light with dark markings and
Smooth like a rock;
Where learning occurs,
I help convey thought.
What am I?

# RIDDLE ME THIS

**PURPOSE:** Establish a Learning Community, Introduce New Concept, Refocus Learner

## SET-UP

- Create a slide that says the following:
    - o Light with dark markings and smooth like a rock, where learning occurs, I help convey thought. What am I?
    - o Text chat your guess.
- Create a second slide that includes the answer: A whiteboard
- Create a slide that includes the following:
    - o I am a source of communication. I am a way of meeting. I wink at you. I am known as the "Great Gossiper." I am intellectual. What am I?
- Create a second slide that includes the answer: A computer
- Insert the slides into the beginning of the presentation or as energizer slides in the middle of the slide deck.

## TRAINER PROCESS

- Put up the "Riddle Me This" slide.
- Ask learners to text chat the answer or ideas as they come up with one.

- When someone has the right answer, move on to the next slide.
- When that has been solved, ask participants to make a connection between the riddles and what is being learned or will be learned.
  - o Look for: tools we will use today; part of how we learn is by writing things down; sometimes we think we are being clear, but the learner may not grasp it
- No matter the riddle, it can be used as a quick way to energize a group and get brain cells firing again.

# PRODUCER PROCESS

- Review answers to riddles and update leader's guide with possible responses that relate.

# VARIATIONS

- Each learner is responsible for coming up with a riddle about a learning theme or topic covered. These need to be emailed to the facilitator prior to the next webinar (along with the answer). Use the "Riddles" throughout the next session to energize learners and revisit content in a fun way.
- Use easier riddles for quicker reaction and response. For more advanced critical thinkers use slightly more complex riddles.
- Tie the riddle to the content whenever possible. Use riddles as a way to transition from one topic to another.

**WEBINAR LENGTH:** > 60 minutes

**ACTIVITY LENGTH:** 5-10 minutes

**INSTRUCTOR SKILL LEVEL:** Novice

**PARTICIPANT SKILL LEVEL:** Novice

**SUPPLIES:** Slide

**TOOLS:** Group Whiteboard

**CLOSER**

LEARNING ACTIVITY

**OPENER**

SOFT OPENER

ENERGIZER

**REVISITER**

# SEEK AND SOLVE

**PURPOSE:** Brainstorm, Establish a Learning Community, Familiarizing, Introduce New Concept, Preview Material, Recall Background Knowledge, Recall Information-Existing Schemas, Review

## SET-UP

- Create an "Objectives" slide that has a list of class objectives as defined by the facilitator.
- Create a "Seek and Solve" slide that has an image of a spyglass as a watermark and the words "seek" in the top left corner and "solve" in the top right corner. Place a vertical line running down the middle of the slide to break the slide evenly into halves.
- Insert the "Objectives" slide at the very beginning of the presentation.
- To use as an opener, insert the "Seek and Solve" slide into the presentation after any opening tool practice slides. To use as a closer, insert this as the last slide before a break or the end of the session.

## TRAINER PROCESS

- Have the "Objectives" slide up as participants enter the virtual meeting room.

- When the "Seek and Solve" slide comes up, have each participant post a question they have about the topic that is about to be covered on the "Seek" portion of the slide.
- After each person posts a question, they will then begin reading the questions and look to answer or "Solve" other people's questions on the "Solve" side of the whiteboard.
- Several of the questions will be answered before formally beginning because of varying knowledge in the virtual room.
- As questions are solved, they are crossed off.
- Throughout the session, jump back to the "Seek and Solve" whiteboard and see if any of the other questions have been answered.
- Each time questions are answered, have learners again respond by writing the answer on the solved side and crossing it off.
- By the end of the session, all "Seeking" questions should be answered on the "Solved" side of the whiteboard.
- If this is being done as a closer, have learners write a question at the very beginning of the session. At the end of the session, close by looking at the slide again and having learners cross off their question if it was answered. If it isn't crossed off, take time to respond or identify a resource to further clarify.

# PRODUCER PROCESS

- If a question has been answered, make sure it is crossed off.
- Capture participants' questions and answers on the whiteboard to add to a Frequently Asked Questions resource for the facilitator.

# VARIATIONS

- If the platform allows for object movement, have learners simply drag the question for which they have an answer to the solved side and either text chat or verbally share the answer.
- If you are short on time or are working with novice users, have them type in their question and highlight or star the questions for which they have answers.

**WEBINAR LENGTH:** Any

**ACTIVITY LENGTH:** 1-5 minutes

**INSTRUCTOR SKILL LEVEL:** Novice

**PARTICIPANT SKILL LEVEL:** Novice

**SUPPLIES:** Slide

**TOOLS:** Polling

CLOSER
**LEARNING ACTIVITY**
**OPENER**
SOFT OPENER
**ENERGIZER**
**REVISITER**

Signal Survey-Polling
Options Highlighted

# SIGNAL SURVEY

**PURPOSE:** Apply Material, Combining, Establish a Learning Community, Familiarizing, Innovate New Ideas, Introduce New Concept, Preview Material, Recall Background Knowledge, Recall Information-Existing Schemas, Refocus Learner, Review, Teach New Material

## SET-UP

- Create a "Signal Survey" slide(s) that has a question and a small screenshot highlighting the polling tool or signal to be used. A signal could be a smiley face or learners could raise their hand or clap to show approval. Questions could relate to pacing, content, level of interest in the subject matter, true/false questions about prior knowledge, yes/no surveys, etc. Create as many question slides as needed.
- Become familiar with signals on the platform you will be using.
- Insert the slides as the first slide if used as an opener to get a pulse on where learners are at with the content. Insert throughout for revisiting or energizing and at any point when used as the learning activity.

# TRAINER PROCESS

- Put up the "Signal Survey" slide.
- Share that this is a question response activity.
- Have learners stand up and stretch while they select their polling answer to the question.
- Turn on your webcam to demonstrate standing up and then model selecting an answer.
- Once everyone has selected their answer, post responses or talk through the overall reaction to the question.
- An example question might be, "Is this process clear?" If you have multiple users frowning, you might poll the audience (see polling in chapter 5) and give them options for responding, or you may go deeper and provide an additional illustration to better clarify the process.

# PRODUCER PROCESS

- Before questions go on the whiteboard, select the correct polling feature.
- Put up the polling results so all can view overall feedback.
- Assist learners with technical difficulties or questions.

# VARIATIONS

- If you need a quick engager and haven't had a chance to prepare a slide, just add a whiteboard and insert a question in the moment.
- In you're in a time crunch, put up a timer for 2 minutes and have learners answer as many poll questions as possible.
- Have learners create their own poll questions by raising their hands and asking or writing on the whiteboard.
- Have participants work in breakout rooms to come up with one polling question per person that reviews the content covered. Once they are done, copy their questions into the main room and use as the polling questions.

**WEBINAR LENGTH:** Any

**ACTIVITY LENGTH:** 5-10 minutes

**INSTRUCTOR SKILL LEVEL:** Novice

**PARTICIPANT SKILL LEVEL:** Novice

**SUPPLIES:** Slide

**TOOLS:** Group Whiteboard

CLOSER
LEARNING ACTIVITY
OPENER
SOFT OPENER
ENERGIZER
REVISITER

# SINGULARLY SPEAKING

**PURPOSE:** Apply Material, Brainstorm, Establish a Learning Community, Familiarizing, Introduce New Concept, Recall Background Knowledge, Recall Information-Existing Schemas, Refocus Learner, Teach New Material

## SET-UP

- Create a slide that includes the following (these can be split into individual slides):
    - o Title: Singularly Speaking
    - o Image in the background of cattle or fish.
- Directions: Whiteboard words that either have no (or a rarely used) singular version. One example is cattle.
- Create a second slide that includes some answers (optional):
    - o Agenda, braces, gold, gear, scissors, pants, trout, swine, fish, salmon, moose, deer, pike, sheep, aircraft, blues, cannon, stone, algae, data, graffiti, paparazzi, tings, pliers, billiards, measles, honesty.
- Insert the slide into the beginning of the presentation. Put up the slide prior to the webinar as a soft opener to help acclimate learners to the platform tools. If this is to be used as an opener, insert the slide at the start of the session. To use this as an energizer, insert the slide anywhere.

# TRAINER PROCESS

- Put up the "Singularly Speaking" slide.
- Ask learners to place their ideas on the whiteboard.
- After 90 seconds, continue to the next content piece if used as an energizer. If used as an opener, ask participants to make a connection between these types of words and what is being learned or will be learned. Have learners raise their hands and turn on their microphones to share.
  - o Look for: only one way to do the process being learned; a lot of ideas when working and brainstorming in a group; team problem-solving goes quicker than doing alone

# PRODUCER PROCESS

- Welcome participants as they enter the virtual room via text chat.
- Whiteboard an idea or two to spur thoughts.
- Turn on timer for 30-60 seconds (variation only).

# VARIATIONS

- Create a slide with a lot of images. Each image must be the visual representation of a noun with no singular form like cattle, pike or algae.
- Use images or words only related to the content.
- Have learners work individually at first to come up with words and then, after 30-60 seconds, have them work together. Debrief with questions like: What helped you to be successful? What does success look like? What insights can we take away from this exercise and apply back at work?
- Tie the word puzzle to the content whenever possible. Use the word puzzle to transition to a new topic.

**WEBINAR LENGTH:** Any

**ACTIVITY LENGTH:** 1-5 minutes

**INSTRUCTOR SKILL LEVEL:** Novice

**PARTICIPANT SKILL LEVEL:** Novice

**SUPPLIES:** Slide

**TOOLS:** Group Text Chat

CLOSER
LEARNING ACTIVITY
OPENER
SOFT OPENER
**ENERGIZER**
REVISITER

# SPORTSMANIA

**PURPOSE:** Establish a Learning Community, Refocus Learner

## SET-UP

- Create a "Sportsmania" slide that includes the following:
    - Images of activities.
    - A selection of the following:
        - Shooting a jump shot
        - Running through tires
        - Batting a baseball
        - Serving a tennis ball
        - Skiing downhill
        - Spiking a volleyball
        - Swinging a golf club
        - Throwing a football
        - Juggling a soccer ball
        - Shooting an arrow
        - Shooting a hockey puck
        - Swimming underwater
        - Dunking a basketball
- Insert the slide anywhere throughout the presentation for fun as an energizer.

# TRAINER PROCESS

- Put up the "Sportsmania" slide when learners are starting to fade.
- Have participants text chat their favorite sport to play or watch and one of the movements done in that sport.
- They can create their own or select one from the slide.
- Then announce that it's time for a "Sportsmania" break. Have them do the motion they chatted for 30-45 seconds to get their blood moving.
- Encourage participation by demonstrating the movements on a webcam.
- After the timer is done, ask participants to text chat how they are feeling now compared to before they took their sports break.

# PRODUCER PROCESS

- Put up timer for 30-45 seconds.

# VARIATIONS

- Put up the list on the screen and have participants change motions every 15 seconds for up to a minute.
- In need of a quick unplanned energizer? Put up a blank whiteboard and have learners post sports. Then they just get up and do that sport for 30 seconds. It is quick and easy to throw in at any time.

**WEBINAR LENGTH:** Any

**ACTIVITY LENGTH:** 2-5 minutes

**INSTRUCTOR SKILL LEVEL:** Novice

**PARTICIPANT SKILL LEVEL:** Novice

**SUPPLIES:** Stickers

**TOOLS:** Text Chat or Two-way Audio

CLOSER
LEARNING ACTIVITY
OPENER
SOFT OPENER
**ENERGIZER**
**REVISITER**

# STICK IT

**PURPOSE:** Apply Material, Brainstorm, Combining, Familiarizing, Review

## SET-UP

- Create a handout titled "Top Takeaways" for participants to write down learnings throughout the webinar.
- Prior to the webinar, send out a welcome package to your participants. Contents should include a welcome letter or confirmation and a page of stickers. The stickers can be colorful or as simple as dots.
- Create a "Stick It" slide that has an image of the sticker sheet with the page number of their "Top Takeaways" page.
- Insert the slide at whatever point needed for engagement or revisiting, or at the end if this is being used as a closer. This slide can be used multiple times during a session at various points.

# TRAINER PROCESS

- Put up the "Stick It" slide.
- Have learners open their workbooks to their "Top Takeaways" page.
- Give 60 seconds to add two to three new learning ideas to their page. Allow a maximum of 60 seconds or you may lose them to email!
- After 60 seconds, have them sticker one idea they want to take action on right away.
- For a quick check to ensure they have found something, have participants text chat (or use two-way audio and share) their best idea.

# PRODUCER PROCESS

- Mail materials and confirmation letter to learner prior to the session.
- Put up timer for 60 seconds.

# VARIATIONS

- Have participants use a marker or highlighter instead of using stickers.
- Have learners raise their hands once they have added four ideas to their page so you know when they are ready to move on. If they have their hand up, they should also stand up and take a quick stretch break.
- When used as a closer, have everyone text chat or whiteboard their best idea.

**WEBINAR LENGTH:** Any

**ACTIVITY LENGTH:** 15 minutes

**INSTRUCTOR SKILL LEVEL:** Intermediate

**PARTICIPANT SKILL LEVEL:** Intermediate

**SUPPLIES:** Slide

**TOOLS:** Breakout Rooms, Group Whiteboard

CLOSER
**LEARNING ACTIVITY**
OPENER
SOFT OPENER
ENERGIZER
**REVISITER**

Team Huddle

Team Leader: Person with the most miles on their car
Task: Brainstorm on whiteboard top takeaways and highlight the group's top three takeaways (modify the task based on the purpose of the activity).

# TEAM HUDDLE

**PURPOSE:** Apply Material, Brainstorm, Combining, Establish a Learning Community, Familiarizing, Innovate New Ideas, Introduce New Concept, Preview Material, Recall Background Knowledge, Recall Information-Existing Schemas, Refocus Learner, Review, Teach New Material

## SET-UP
- Create a handout titled "Top Takeaways" for participants to write down learnings throughout the webinar.
- Create a slide that includes the following:
    - o Title: Team Huddle
    - o Team moderator is the person with the most miles on their car
    - o Task: Brainstorm top takeaways and highlight the group's top three takeaways (modify the task based on the purpose of the activity).
- Insert the slide into the presentation partway through the webinar to revisit, before a break or at the very end as a closer and anywhere throughout as needed for brainstorming, collecting new ideas, etc.

# TRAINER PROCESS

- Have learners turn to their "Top Takeaways" page or the content page being worked on.
- Put up the "Team Huddle" slide.
- Share that groups will be put into breakout rooms in just a moment. If this is a closer, each group is to brainstorm concepts that have resonated with each person. If this is being used as a learning activity, have learners work together to accomplish the task.
- Have participants write these on their whiteboards using the webinar platform tools (different colors, drawing tools, text, etc.). Allow 3-4 minutes for this.
- The team moderator will stop the group when there is 1 minute left and have team members vote on the top three ideas brainstormed.
- Have all groups come back together and the teams' moderators will share their whiteboard with the group. Any ideas that are duplicated do not need to be covered again.
- Have participants add to their "Top Takeaways" page in their workbooks while groups are sharing.

# PRODUCER PROCESS

- Create breakout rooms.
- Post pre-made slide in breakout rooms with instructions.
- Put up a timer for 3-4 minutes and have it count down.
- Answer any questions that come through via text chat.
- Check in on breakout rooms and answer any questions.
- Post breakout room whiteboards in the main room for viewing or application share the whiteboards.

# VARIATIONS

- With small groups, do this in the main room together.
- Have small groups focus on one topic area and brainstorm all key learning points from that section of content.

**WEBINAR LENGTH:** Any

**ACTIVITY LENGTH:** 1-5 minutes

**INSTRUCTOR SKILL LEVEL:** Novice

**PARTICIPANT SKILL LEVEL:** Novice

**SUPPLIES:** Pre-made Slide, Piece of Paper per Participant

**TOOLS:** Polling

CLOSER
LEARNING ACTIVITY
OPENER
SOFT OPENER
**ENERGIZER**
REVISITER

# TRASH COLLECTOR

**PURPOSE:** Establishing a Learning Community, Refocus Learner

## SET-UP

- Create a slide that includes the following:
  - o Title: Trash Collector
  - o An image of a garbage can or garbage truck in the background.
  - o List out the following:
    - Elbow and elbow
    - Foot and foot
    - Knee and knee
    - Forearm and elbow
    - Foot and elbow
    - Knee and elbow
    - Forehead and back of hand
    - Toe and finger
- Insert the slide anywhere throughout the presentation for fun as an energizer.

# TRAINER PROCESS

- Put up the "Trash Collector" direction slide when learners start to fade.
- Have participants locate a piece of scrap paper and crumple it into a ball.
- Each participant stands up and locates a spot across the room or outside their cube. This spot becomes their imaginary trash can.
- Each person tries to toss their paper ball and hit their trash can.
- If they make the shot, they raise their virtual hand. They are "free" to pick up their garbage and sit back in their chair.
- If, however, they miss their garbage can, they get to collect their trash in one of the optional ways listed on the slide.
- Encourage participation by demonstrating the movements on a webcam.
- After everyone has retrieved their garbage, have learners use an emoticon or icon to show how they are feeling.

# PRODUCER PROCESS

- Put on webcam and participate.
- Keep track of team points (variation only).

# VARIATIONS

- Want competition? Split the learners into teams. Make teams fun–guys vs. gals, East Coast vs. West Coast, and so on. Do the trash collector energizer two to three times in a row with participants identifying new "trash cans" each time. If the learner makes the shot, they get one point. If the learner misses and collects the trash in the way the facilitator randomly selects, they get two points. Use this activity multiple times throughout the session; in the second half of the session, learners earn double points.
- Imagine the trash is really a treasure such as a wadded up deed to a house or a $20,000 check. Now retrieve it and smooth it out using one of the aforementioned ways.

**WEBINAR LENGTH:** Any

**ACTIVITY LENGTH:** 5-10 minutes

**INSTRUCTOR SKILL LEVEL:** Novice

**PARTICIPANT SKILL LEVEL:** Intermediate

**SUPPLIES:** Slide

**TOOLS:** Group Whiteboard, Group Text Chat

CLOSER
LEARNING ACTIVITY
OPENER
SOFT OPENER
**ENERGIZER**
**REVISITER**

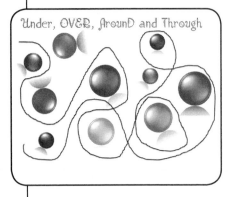

# UNDER, OVER, AROUND AND THROUGH

**PURPOSE:** Recall Background Knowledge, Recall Information-Existing Schemas, Refocus Learner, Review

## SET-UP

- Create an "Under, Over, Around and Through" slide that includes the following:
    - o Multiple images of objects randomly placed with space between images. Place some of the images close together to increase difficulty of the activity. Images can be anything from products a company sells to fun, playful pictures.
    - o Draw a line weaving up, down and all around the objects but not touching any of them.
- Insert the slide after content is covered to revisit or anywhere throughout for fun as an energizer.

## TRAINER PROCESS

- Put up the "Under, Over, Around and Through" slide.
- Ask learners to use their drawing tools and move around the obstacles following the pre-made line denoting the path.

- The first person to make it through the obstacle course wins a small prize.
- If anyone "hits" or touches an obstacle along the way, they get to text chat one thing they have learned so far during the session (revisiter only).
- Demonstrate using a drawing tool and start the course. Purposely hit an object and text chat something learned.
- As comments are texted, read off what was written (revisiter only).

## PRODUCER PROCESS

- Put up the timer (variation only).

## VARIATIONS

- Put learners' names on the slide and associate each with a color; announce the race and who is in the lead as participants finagle their way through.
- Make it a race against time. Put up the slide a second time and see if learners can beat their original time.
- Leave out the pre-drawn line and have the facilitator draw the line in the moment while participants follow as quickly and accurately as possible.

**WEBINAR LENGTH:** Multiple Session

**ACTIVITY LENGTH:** 5 Minutes, Multiple Times

**INSTRUCTOR SKILL LEVEL:** Intermediate

**PARTICIPANT SKILL LEVEL:** Novice

**SUPPLIES:** Slide

**TOOLS:** Two-way Audio, Whiteboard

CLOSER
LEARNING ACTIVITY
**OPENER**
SOFT OPENER
**ENERGIZER**
**REVISITER**

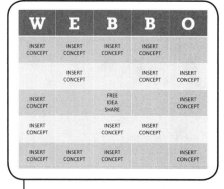

# WEBB"O"

**PURPOSE:** Combining, Familiarizing, Introduce New Concept, Preview Material, Recall Background Knowledge, Recall Information-Existing Schemas, Refocus Learner, Review

## SET-UP

- Create a "WEBBO" slide that has a sample WEBBO (bingo) card.
- Create a "WEBBO Words" slide that includes terms not already on the WEBBO board, which participants will use to fill in the empty spots on their card. Have more terms than blank spaces.
- Create a homemade WEBBO (bingo) card, which is a 5x5 grid. Fill 19 of the 25 spaces with concepts to be covered throughout the webinar sessions. The center space is a free space.
- Add printed WEBBO cards to your materials list to mail or email to participants prior to the session.
- Insert the slide at the beginning and throughout the session multiple times to remind the participants about the game.

## TRAINER PROCESS

- Put up the "WEBBO Words" slide.
- As learners log into the session, have them fill in the blanks with ideas from the slide. One idea per blank.
- Give 2½ minutes for learners to fill in their blanks.

**150**

- Share the following WEBBO Rules:
  - o As topics are randomly covered, learners will cross off the topic and write one thing they learned about it in the proper box.
  - o When a participant has completed the specified WEBBO pattern, such as five boxes in a row vertically, horizontally or diagonally, they raise their hand and text chat WEBBO.
  - o Before receiving the prize, the learner must share one learning they had for each square in the winning pattern.
  - o Before you continue on with new material, announce the next pattern for WEBBO. Other patterns can include four corners, the shape of a capital T or H, or blackout the board with every space covered. Insert the WEBBO card slide as the last slide to be used as the final closer.
- Prizes are awarded to each participant as they get WEBBO and share three or four of their blanks with the group.
- If this is being used as a closer, pair up the learners and have them share any three boxes they have filled in and what they learned in that content piece.

## PRODUCER PROCESS

- Mail/email out WEBBO cards prior to the session.
- Put up timer for 2 1/2 minutes.
- Watch text chat for questions.
- Send out prizes awarded to participants after the session.

## VARIATIONS

- The WEBBO card can be uploaded to the platform and downloaded and printed by each participant.
- To increase the challenge, create four versions with only 16 spaces pre-filled. Create a slide with the remaining terms and let participants choose in which boxes to place concepts.
- For a shorter webinar, play "WEB" and create a 3x3 grid with nine spaces.

**WEBINAR LENGTH:** Any

**ACTIVITY LENGTH:** 5 minutes

**INSTRUCTOR SKILL LEVEL:** Novice

**PARTICIPANT SKILL LEVEL:** Novice

**SUPPLIES:** Slide

**TOOLS:** Group Text Chat

CLOSER
LEARNING ACTIVITY
OPENER
SOFT OPENER
**ENERGIZER**
**REVISITER**

Who done it? Unlock the mystery...

# WHO DONE IT?

**PURPOSE:** Refocus Learner, Review

## SET-UP

- Create a "Who Done It?" slide that has clues to a piece of content. Reveal one clue at a time if the platform allows for animation. If not, have clues prepared in advance and type them on the whiteboard one at a time. Prepare multiple clues and pilot test to ensure enough clues are created.
- Create additional slides if you're having learners guess multiple content areas. One slide per content or topic.
- Insert the slide(s) at whatever point needed for engagement and revisit or at the end if a closer.

## TRAINER PROCESS

- Put up the "Who Done It" slide.
- Share that this is a game of sleuthing. Participants will need to grab their detective caps, pipes and magnifying glasses to determine which piece of content or data was covered.
- Reveal information one click at a time about a given topic on the whiteboard. If this feature isn't available, just type in the clues.

- For ease, prepare the clues in advance in a word document and copy and paste them in to keep things moving.
- Participants watch the clues, both written and visual, and take guesses in the text chat area of the webinar.
- The first person to guess correctly wins a small prize or points that can be collected throughout the session.
- When someone has the right answer, move on to the next slide.
- Once learners have guessed the content, have each text chat one takeaway they have for that lesson. What will they try first? What was their biggest learning?

# PRODUCER PROCESS

- Process winners and mail/email prizes as necessary.
- Watch text chatting area for correct answers.
- Create breakout rooms (variation only).
- Post the pre-made slide in breakout rooms with instructions (variation only).
- Put up a timer for 5-10 minutes and have it count down (variation only).
- Answer any questions that come through via text chat (variation only).
- Check in on breakout rooms and answer any questions (variation only).

# VARIATIONS

- Have learners go into breakout rooms and create clues for a piece of content covered. Allow for 5-10 minutes for their discussion and brainstorming. When everyone is back in the main room, have each group reveal their clues one at a time and see how quickly others guess their topic.
- Give learners clues for being back on time from breaks or lunch. At the end of the session, use this as a closer. Those that have the additional clues will get the answer quicker, winning a small prize.

# APPENDIX A
## WEBINAR PLATFORMS FOR TRAINING

A list of all vendors that support a collaborative online teaching platform with a combination of synchronous classroom features.

**Adobe Acrobat Connect Pro** – Adobe.com, 1-888-649-2990
**Elluminate 9.7** – Elluminate.com, 1-800-GO-ELLUMINATE
**GoToTraining™** – GoToMeeting.com, 1-888-646-0014
**iLinc** – iLinc.com, 1-800-767-9054
**Live Meeting** – Microsoft.com, 1-866-463-3866
**Nefsis®** – Nefsis.com, 1-858-715-0970
**Saba Centra Suite** – Saba.com, 1-781-861-7000
**WebEx** – WebEx.com, 1-877-509-3239

# APPENDIX B
## ADDIE MODEL OVERVIEW FOR WEBINARS

|  | ANALYZE | DESIGN |
|---|---|---|
| **TACTICS** | Spending time with the client to transfer knowledge and ask key questions such as:<br>o Who is the audience?<br>o What webinar experience do they have?<br>o What do they need to learn?<br>o What constraints exist?<br>o What is the timeline for project completion?<br>o What other systems or best methods will this change impact?<br>o How do we define "success"? | Building a blueprint of the training program.<br>o Defining learning objectives<br>o Determining course content<br>o Determining instructional strategies and methods<br>o Determining the evaluation approach<br>o Documenting resource requirements (e.g. funding, time, personnel, equipment, etc.) |
| **MEETING EXAMPLES** | o Process Flow<br>o Business Scenario/Use Case<br>o Business User Reviews<br>o Usability Labs<br>o Needs Assessment Interviews | o Course outline review<br>o Training design review |
| **% OF TIME NEEDED** | 25% | 20% |

| DEVELOP | IMPLEMENT | EVALUATE |
|---|---|---|
| The actual "construction" of elements that will support the training program.<br>o Course materials<br>o Learning activities<br>o Lesson plan and trainer's guide<br>o Tests or other assessment materials<br>o Job aids | The point at which the training plan is finally developed and delivered. This plan consists of:<br>o "Dry Run" webinar (e.g. pilot)<br>o Updates and revisions to the webinar training following the dry run<br>o Finalization of training<br>o Train-the-trainer sessions (if needed)<br>o Roll out the live webinar course | Systemic process that determines the quality and effectiveness of the training as well as the final product.<br>o Did we meet our objectives?<br>o Did the learning experience add value?<br>o Like It (Level 1): Assesses the participants' initial reactions to the training course.<br>o Learn It (Level 2): Assesses the amount of information that participants learned.<br>o Use It (Level 3): Assesses whether or not the participant was able to transfer the learning and apply on the job (6 weeks to 6 months post-training).<br>o Impact (Level 4): Assesses the financial impact of the training course related to ROI (6 months to 2 years post-training). |
| o Periodic content-review meetings | o Dry-run webinar<br>o Final logistics-review meeting(s)<br>o Final content-review meeting(s)<br>o Live webinar session | o Pilot/Roll out feedback sessions<br>o Roll out postmortem<br>o Post-training feedback development and update |
| 35% | 15% | 5% |

# APPENDIX C
## RESOURCES

### BOOKS
*ASTD Handbook for Workplace Learning Professionals*
  Elaine Biech, ASTD Press, 2008.
*Creative Training Techniques Handbook*
  Bob Pike, Lakewood Publications, 3rd Edition, 2002.
*Designing Web-Based Training*
  William Horton, John Wiley & Sons, 2000.
*Elearning and the Science of Instruction: Proven Guidelines for Consumers and Designers of Multimedia Learning*
  Ruth C. Clark and Richard E. Mayer, Pfeiffer, 2007.
*Elearning by Design*
  William Horton, Pfeiffer, 2006.
*Evaluating Training Programs: The Four Levels*
  Donald L. Kirkpatrick, Berrett-Koehler Publishers, 2nd Edition,1998.
*Instructional Systems Development: An Info-line Collection*
  ASTD Editors, ASTD Press, 2007.
*Live and Online!: Tips, Techniques and Ready-to-Use Activities for the Virtual Classroom*
  Jennifer Hofmann, Pfeiffer, 2004.
*The Trainer's Balanced Scorecard*
  Ajay M. Pangarkar and Teresa Kirkwood, Pfeiffer, 2009.
*The Trainers Handbook Updated Edition*
  Karen Lawson, Pfeiffer, 2008.

### WEBSITES
These links include information about training and development, ranging from elearning to classroom training. All links were active at printing, but can break or be terminated at any time as they are not owned by Pluth Consulting. These sites are for informational purposes and do not reflect endorsement.

- ASTD.org
  *American Society for Training & Development (ASTD)*
  The world's largest association dedicated to workplace learning and performance professionals. ASTD's members come from more than 100 countries. Members work in thousands of organizations of all sizes, in government, as independent consultants and suppliers.

- **BobPikeGroup.com**
  *The Bob Pike Group*
  Provides training workshops and consulting services for both classroom and online training.
- **Brandon-Hall.com**
  *Brandon Hall Research*
  Provides useful elearning and distance learning information.
- **CreativeTrainingTech.com**
  *Creative Training Techniques Newsletter*
  This monthly digital newsletter has dozens of tips, tactics and how-to's for delivering effective training. For managers, training professionals, supervisors, executives or anyone who trains. A professional resource to improve and maximize training.
- **FreeMind.sourceforge.net**
  FreeMind is a free mind-mapping software written in Java.
- **LearningWare.com**
  *LearningWare*
  This company has several products which can make training more engaging including AllPlay Web and Gameshow Pro, a software tool that allows trainers and instructors to create and play different Hollywood-style game shows in any training space.
- **Masie.com**
  *Masie Center*
  Home of the Learning Consortium, the Masie Center is an international think tank dedicated to exploring the intersection of learning and technology.
- **PuzzleMaker.school.discovery.com**
  Puzzlemaker is a puzzle generation tool for teachers, students and parents. Create and print customized word search, criss-cross, math puzzles, and more using your own word lists.

- TurningTechnologies.com
  *Turning Technologies*
  TurningPoint audience response system integrates 100 percent into Microsoft® PowerPoint® and allows audiences and students to participate in presentations or lectures by submitting responses to interactive questions using a ResponseCard® keypad or other hand-held/computer devices.
- Qwizdom.com
  *Qwizdom, Inc*
  This company provides interactive data-gathering solutions for corporations, schools and government agencies around the world. Qwizdom offers an advanced radio-frequency audience response technology where everyone in the room participates and provides instant feedback to the presenter.
- LearnCentral.org
  This social network for those who do webinars allows users to upload and download activities and slide decks with examples of exercises, and ask questions of one another as it pertains to synchronous training.
- Horton.com
  *William Horton Consulting, Inc.*
  Elearning design specialists with a wealth of industry knowledge and resources.

# APPENDIX D
## BEFORE, DURING AND AFTER CHECKLIST

| BEFORE THE SESSION | DURING THE SESSION | AFTER THE SESSION |
|---|---|---|
| o prepare thoroughly<br><br>o be familiar with the software<br><br>o know your content<br><br>o create strong objectives<br><br>o prepare to teach in the online medium<br><br>o create closers, openers, revisiters and energizers<br><br>o have a backup plan<br><br>o experience it as a participant<br><br>o follow the four P's – plan, prepare, practice, perform<br><br>o select captains or champions for the training<br><br>o assess your audience<br><br>o create active learning activities<br><br>o host a pre-elearning session to make sure trainees know how to log on and be successful with the interface | o start and end on time<br><br>o open the e-meeting room early<br><br>o provide printed handbooks for learners to work in<br><br>o give and receive feedback<br><br>o correct learners effectively<br><br>o allow/plan for silence<br><br>o problems will arise, be flexible<br><br>o stay organized<br><br>o engage your audience<br><br>o have a subject matter expert (SME) in the room<br><br>o have two computers running so you can also log in as a student<br><br>o plan for revisit and reuse | o follow up with participants on parking lot items<br><br>o bridge the content gap with an email or voicemail<br><br>o provide IT support for users<br><br>o enhance the content and curriculum<br><br>o hold a postmortem with key stakeholders to share successes and learnings |

# APPENDIX E
## TASKS REQUIRED TO DESIGN, PRODUCE AND DELIVER A PARTICIPANT-CENTERED WEBINAR

| CHECKLIST | TEAM MEMBER RESPONSIBLE | DUE DATE | DONE | N/A |
|---|---|---|---|---|
| Analysis | | | | |
| Identify knowledge, skills, attitudes | | | | |
| Draft needs assessment | | | | |
| Administer assessment | | | | |
| Analyze assessment data | | | | |
| Determine depth of knowledge needed | | | | |
| Webinar Objectives | | | | |
| Write business objective | | | | |
| Write manager objective | | | | |
| Write learner objective | | | | |
| Define project scope | | | | |
| Write session description | | | | |
| Course Set-up | | | | |
| Identify/purchase webinar platform | | | | |
| Create invitation link | | | | |
| Secure conference bridge number/VoIP | | | | |
| Set pilot date/time | | | | |
| Set roll out date/time | | | | |
| Select trainer | | | | |
| Select producer | | | | |
| Select champions or captains | | | | |
| Evaluation | | | | |
| Determine level 1-4 (Kirkpatrick) evaluation criteria | | | | |
| Write objectives for module 1 | | | | |
| Write objectives for module 2 | | | | |
| Write objectives for module 3 | | | | |
| Write objectives for module 4 | | | | |

| CHECKLIST | TEAM MEMBER RESPONSIBLE | DUE DATE | DONE | N/A |
|---|---|---|---|---|
| Write objectives for module 5 | | | | |
| Write objectives for module 6 | | | | |
| Design Session | | | | |
| Brainstorm content | | | | |
| Chunk content | | | | |
| Schedule physical break every 60-90 minutes | | | | |
| Identify webinar tools available | | | | |
| Create job aids | | | | |
| Define and create pre-work | | | | |
| Select or develop soft openers, openers and closers | | | | |
| Select or develop energizers and revisit activities | | | | |
| Identify and develop follow-up materials | | | | |
| Select additional media to use: music/video/articles | | | | |
| Determine breakout rooms/groups | | | | |
| Develop all components** for module 1 | | | | |
| Develop all components**for module 2 | | | | |
| Develop all components** for module 3 | | | | |
| Develop all components** for module 4 | | | | |
| Develop all components** for module 5 | | | | |
| Develop all components** for module 6 | | | | |

*\*Webinar interactive activities can be done using the following tools: whiteboard, quizzes, polling, text chat, application sharing, webcam, VoIP, breakout, recordings, videos and asynchronous games.*

| CHECKLIST | TEAM MEMBER RESPONSIBLE | DUE DATE | DONE | N/A |
|---|---|---|---|---|
| Develop leader's guide with producer notes | | | | |
| Create games and exercises housed online for asynchronous use | | | | |
| Develop a backup plan for activities | | | | |
| Create level 1 session evaluation | | | | |
| Design slide deck content | | | | |
| Create handouts/learner workbook | | | | |
| Draft registration information | | | | |
| Identify participant download | | | | |
| Develop participant packing list for mailing (email/post) | | | | |
| Purchase supplies/materials for session and mailing | | | | |
| Develop mailings/invitations<br>• Welcome letter<br>• Platform instructions with session link<br>• Supplies for session<br>• Pre-work assignments | | | | |
| Production/Layout | | | | |
| Complete layout of slides | | | | |
| Complete production of video clips | | | | |
| Complete production of audio clips | | | | |
| Complete layout of leader's guide | | | | |
| Complete layout of handouts | | | | |
| Create PDF of all participant materials | | | | |

| CHECKLIST | TEAM MEMBER RESPONSIBLE | DUE DATE | DONE | N/A |
|---|---|---|---|---|
| Communication | | | | |
| Send mailings/invitations | | | | |
| Send invitation reminder | | | | |
| Review class roster | | | | |
| Send out follow-up materials after session | | | | |
| Practice | | | | |
| Examine all content | | | | |
| Practice all tools on platform | | | | |
| Record practice and review | | | | |
| Experience session as a learner | | | | |
| Make revisions to session | | | | |
| Support | | | | |
| Verify IT support | | | | |
| Reserve second computer | | | | |
| Producer practice session | | | | |
| Contact information for conference call/webinar platform | | | | |
| Print webinar platform FAQ and quick-reference guides | | | | |

# APPENDIX F
## DESIGN TEMPLATES

**Webinar Session Name:** _____  **Form copyright 2010 Pluth Consulting**

| | | | | |
|---|---|---|---|---|
| **ID** | Description | Scope | Trainer | Webinar Information<br>Invitation Link:<br>Conference Bridge Number:<br>Date:<br>Time: |
| | | | | Manager Objective |
| **Objectives** | Business Objective | Learner Objective | | |
| **Team** | Trainer Role | Producer Role | Learner Role | Production |
| | | | | PPT:<br>Slides:<br>Websites to visit: |
| **Resources** | Materials<br>Pre-work:<br>Mailings:<br>Handouts:<br>Slides:<br>Whiteboard Activities:<br>Video:<br>Audio Bridge:<br>Documents: | Content Expert Resources | Follow Up Contact Information | Product Information<br>Tools:<br>Programs:<br>Platform Contact: |

# Webinar Session Planning Checklist

Webinar Title: _____  Trainer: _____  General Description _____  Form copyright 2010 Pluth Consulting

## Session Info / Administration

**Registration**
- ☐ Invitation Sent
- ☐ Online
- ☐ Phone
- ☐ Internal
- ☐ Paper
- ☐ Recorded Session
- ☐ _____
- ☐ _____

**Billing**
- ☐ Free
- ☐ Cost Center # _____
- ☐ Per Learner
- ☐ Per Session
- ☐ _____
- ☐ _____

**Documents Used**
- ☐ Handouts
- ☐ Activity Log
- ☐ Polling
- ☐ Questions
- ☐ Recorded Session
- ☐ Feedback
- ☐ Forms
- ☐ Tests
- ☐ Quizzes

**Security**
- ☐ Open Session
- ☐ Closed Session
- ☐ Guest Invitations

**Follow-up**
- ☐ Completion Email
- ☐ Certificate
- ☐ _____
- ☐ _____
- ☐ _____
- ☐ _____
- ☐ _____

## Communication

**E-mail**
- ☐ Trainer to Learner
- ☐ Learner to Learner
- ☐ Platform to Learner
- ☐ Invitation _____
- ☐ Reminder _____
- ☐ Handouts

**Mailings**
- ☐ Welcome Letter
- ☐ Instructions
- ☐ Handouts
- ☐ Supplies for Session
- ☐ Assignments

**Web-Conference Tools**
- ☐ Text Chat
- ☐ Audio Conference
- ☐ Bridge
- ☐ VoIP
- ☐ Whiteboard
- ☐ Breakouts
- ☐ Application Sharing
- ☐ Polling
- ☐ Video Conference
- ☐ Web Hunt
- ☐ _____

## Webinar Features and Plans

**Assessments**
- ☐ Polling
- ☐ Yes/No
- ☐ Multiple Choice A-C
- ☐ Multiple Choice A-D
- ☐ Multiple Choice A-E
- ☐ Speed
- ☐ Pre-test
- ☐ Post-test

**Evaluation**
- ☐ Pre-test
- ☐ Post-test
- ☐ Session Feedback
- ☐ 30/60/90 Day
- ☐ Follow-up

**Course Announcements**
- ☐ Session Announcement
- ☐ Session Description
- ☐ Session Objectives
- ☐ Registration Information
- ☐ Technical Requirements for Computer
- ☐ About the Trainer

**Support**
- ☐ Producer
- ☐ FAQ checklist
- ☐ Leader's Guide
- ☐ Second Computer

**Test**
- ☐ Platform
- ☐ Slides
- ☐ Hyperlinks
- ☐ Websites

**Resources**
- ☐ Books
- ☐ Terms
- ☐ Downloads
- ☐ Handouts

**NOTES:**

167

**Webinar Session Activity Planner**                                          Form copyright 2010 Pluth Consulting

| Session Info | | |
|---|---|---|

**Webinar Title:** 

**Trainer** 

**General Description** 

**Activity Directions** 

**Whiteboard Slide or Application Screenshot** 

**Activity Information**

| Time | Group Size | Materials Needed | Resources | NOTES: |
|---|---|---|---|---|
| | | | | |

# APPENDIX G
## SAMPLE EVALUATION QUESTIONS AND SCALES

**General Instructor/Producer Questions**
Scale- Strongly Agree, Somewhat Agree, Agree, Somewhat Disagree, Strongly Disagree
- The instructor demonstrated knowledge of content
- The instructor effectively managed the classroom (e.g. set clear expectations, kept class on task, covered all materials, etc.)
- The producer effectively managed the online platform (e.g. transitions to breakout rooms, application sharing, technical support)
- The instructor created a comfortable learning environment (e.g., open to questions, responsive, etc.)
- The instructor adapted learning styles to meet individuals' needs
- The instructor delivered materials at an appropriate pace
- The instructor was knowledgeable about the materials
- The instructor followed through on commitments (e.g., follow-up items, parking lot questions, etc.)

Scale- Very Good, Good, Average, Fair, Poor
- Rate the effectiveness of the instructor

**General Materials Questions**
Scale- Strongly Agree, Somewhat Agree, Agree, Somewhat Disagree, Strongly Disagree
- The materials were (insert any of the following terms: engaging, professional in appearance, current, well-organized, appropriate length, thorough, appropriately challenging, etc.)
- There was an adequate balance of lecture and activity
- The activities were appropriate for meeting the objectives
- Examples help me better understand concepts presented in class (e.g., calls, scenarios, mock calls, etc.)

Scale- Open Ended
- Overall additional comments or suggestions about the materials
- Overall additional comments or suggestions about the instructor

**General Review/Assessment Questions**

**Scale-** Strongly Agree, Somewhat Agree, Agree, Somewhat Disagree, Strongly Disagree

- The webinar environment was conducive to learning
- I was able to use computer resources when necessary (e.g., IT/Producer was available, there were enough computers, systems were accessible)
- Practice time was effective
- There was adequate review time throughout the training
- The review activities were helpful

**Scale-** Extremely Satisfied, Somewhat Satisfied, Satisfied, Somewhat Dissatisfied, Extremely Dissatisfied

- How satisfied were you with the training session

# APPENDIX H
## CHECKLIST FOR CO-FACILITATION

Prior to the Session
_ Individually prepare by reviewing the session to analyze:
  _ The session objectives
  _ The objectives of each module
  _ The key points and activities for each module
_ Schedule ample time for planning either in person or on the phone
_ Take some time to get to know each other
_ Discuss each other's style of planning and facilitating
_ Take time to discuss your views about the session topic and come to
  a common understanding on:
  _ Key objectives of each module
  _ Key points to cover in each module
  _ The process or adult learning methods used in each module
  _ Problems encountered facilitating the course before and how to
    avoid them
  _ How you will divide your tasks and roles (fairly)
_ Examine areas of disagreement
_ Discuss any concerns about potential challenges that participants
  may present
_ Review each other's triggers
_ Discuss how to best interject a thought if not on 'stage'
_ Decide how to keep track of time and a discreet signal to use with
  one another to reference time
_ Strategize about how to stick to the original outline and how to
  transition
_ List what should be prepared in advance and who will do it
_ List what materials need to be mailed to participants or downloaded
  during the session and who will do it
_ Agree on a log-in time for the session for set up and check-in before
  the session begins
_ Schedule time after the workshop to debrief
_ Review each other's triggers
_ Discuss what each of you will do while the other is taking the lead
  in facilitating. This could include observing the dynamics in the
  room, text chatting responses to questions, getting ready for your
  next section, etc.

_ Agree not to contradict, interrupt or correct one another in front of the participants. Find a time during break or when participants are working on an exercise to raise questions or concerns with your co-facilitator.

**Dealing with Difficult … Co-Trainers!**
_ Be mindful of your differences and take them into account in developing your co-facilitating plan
_ Differences include:
    _ Sector of the union or geographic region
    _ Gender
    _ Race
    _ Education
    _ Experience
_ Discuss how you will respond if participants start to favor one of the facilitators because of these differences
_ Honestly discuss your strengths and weaknesses in facilitating this session
_ Decide how to support each other to take advantage of your respective strengths and to improve or overcome your respective weaknesses

**During the Session**
_ Trust and respect each other as equal partners
_ Know your roles and responsibilities and follow through
_ Check in with one another throughout the session
_ Support one another
_ Listen to your co-facilitator and the workshop participants even when you're not "on"
_ Help each other keep on schedule
_ Check in at breaks to see how things are going, how your co-facilitator is feeling and whether any adjustments need to be made
_ Be flexible
_ Learn from your co-facilitator's style
_ Use private text chatting
_ Assert yourself if your co-facilitator is talking too much
_ Remember that it is okay to make mistakes

_ Take the initiative to step in if your co-facilitator misses an opportunity to address something
_ If not facilitating, act as a participant
_ Leverage the strength of styles, presentation and facilitation energy

**After the Session**
_ Listen carefully to one another's self-evaluation before giving feedback
_ Discuss what worked well
_ Examine what did not work
_ Brainstorm what could have been done differently
_ Be honest and respectful of each other as equal partners in co-facilitating when providing feedback, especially if you feel there were problems
_ Use written evaluations as a reference point to talk about the session, and assess your effectiveness as co-facilitators
_ Realize the importance and potential difficulty of debriefing a challenging workshop

# APPENDIX I
## SYNCHRONOUS GLOSSARY

**Annotate** – During a webinar when trainer, producer or participant use drawing or text tools on the whiteboard.

**Application Sharing** – Participants view instructor's documents and applications. Facilitators can also request permission to view a participant's computer applications and desktop.

**Asynchronous Learning** – Learning done alone with no time or location restraints. Available 24/7. A self-paced program typically done with a mobile device or computer.

**Bandwidth** – Speed of data transfer via network or modem using the internet. The greater the bandwidth the faster the computer reads information and gets it to the end user.

**Breakout Sessions** – Tool used to create subgroups in a webinar much like a small group discussion in a classroom or meeting. Learners can go in and connect with a few participants and then be returned to the main room and rejoin the large group.

**Closer** – An activity that ties things together and revisits the content.

**Computer Based Learning** – Computer aided learning (CD-ROM or online via the internet).

**eLearning** – The use of information and computer technologies to create learning experiences.

**Energizer** – An activity that helps get blood flowing and brains thinking. Best used when energy is low. Does not have to be relevant to the content.

**Evaluation** – A feedback form that allows for a trainer to collect information and assess the session content, materials, trainer and participant-engagement levels. Some are done using polling features, some are digital and automatically tabulated and others are produced in a paper-pencil fashion.

**Hyperlinks** – A function that allows a user to click the link and be placed in another section of a document or web page.

**Internet** – Usually the world wide web, but can also be email and file sharing.

**Intranet** – Hosted by a company for its internal use. Not accessible to the public, although it can contain links to the internet.

**Learning Activity** – An interaction that allows the facilitator to teach as the activity progresses. It takes the place of a lecture.

**Opener** – An activity that encourages networking and breaks preoccupation. An opener is relevant to the content; in this way, it is different from an icebreaker.

**Pacing** – Feature that helps instructors know if their speed of content delivery is too fast or slow.

**Playback** – Allows for the webinar session to be recorded and reviewed at a later date.

**Polling** – A synchronous tool that allows for answering questions using polling buttons. Questions come in the form of yes/no, true/false, multiple choice and short answer. Other quick ways to poll are to use emoticons, hand raising and other icons that vary from one webinar platform to another.

**Revisiter** – A revisit is when the learner interacts with content already covered. A review is when the facilitator interacts with content already covered.

**Soft Opener** – This activity engages the audience, sets the tone, puts the attendees at ease, and allows learners to practice using platform tools before the official start of the webinar. It is relevant to the content.

**Text Chat** – Real-time conversation between participants and instructor that is done by text. Text chat is in most platforms and can be programmed to allow private chatting or only public chatting capabilities.

**Two-way Audio** – Any means by which individuals can talk to one another whether it is via the internet or a conference call bridge. In one-way audio, only the trainer can speak.

**Video Conference** – A live teleconference conducted via television equipment or desktop computer via a network or webinar platform.

**VoIP** – Digitally sending the voice over the internet. Stands for 'Voice over Internet Protocol.'

**Webcam** – A digital camera capable of sharing live video feed and images over the internet or webinar platform.

**Whiteboard** – Tool used in webinars to share content, materials and information real-time with others. Most allow for annotation and can be modified in the moment. All learners can view the whiteboard.

# INDEX

| | | | Type of Interaction | | | | | | Tools Required | | | | | | |
| --- | --- | --- | --- | --- | --- | --- | --- | --- | --- | --- | --- | --- | --- | --- | --- |
| | Name | Page | C | L | O | S | E | R | Group Text Chat | 2-way Audio | Group White-board | White-board | Break Out Rooms | App Share | Poll |
| Establishing a Learning Community | ATZRR | 64 | x | | x | | | x | | | x | | | | |
| | BRAVO! | 66 | x | x | x | x | x | x | | x | | | | x | |
| | Bursting Balloons | 68 | x | | x | | | x | | | x | | x | | |
| | Chart Chase | 72 | x | | | | | x | | | x | | | | |
| | Chart Chase 2 | 74 | x | | | | | x | | | | x | | | |
| | Double Trouble | 80 | | | x | x | x | | | | x | | | | |
| | Group Work | 92 | | x | | | | | x | x | | | x | | |
| | Heart Smart | 94 | | | | | x | | | | | | | | x |
| | I Object | 96 | | x | | | | | | x | x | | x | | |
| | Literary Assumptions | 104 | x | x | x | x | x | | | | x | | | | |
| | Map It! | 106 | | | x | x | x | | x | | x | | | | |
| | Mastermind Mix | 108 | | | x | | x | | | x | | | x | | |
| | Pass It On-UNO™Style | 114 | | | | | x | | | | | x | | | |
| | Pesky Palindromes | 116 | | | x | x | x | | x | | | | | | |
| | Pop Ups | 120 | | x | | x | x | | x | x | | | | | x |
| | Q it Up | 122 | x | | x | | x | x | | | x | | | | |
| | ResponseWare | 128 | x | x | x | x | x | x | | x | | | | x | |
| | Reversible Reflection | 130 | | | x | x | x | | x | | | | | | |
| | Riddle Me This | 132 | | | x | x | x | | x | | | | | | |
| | Seek and Solve | 134 | x | | x | | | x | | | x | | | | |
| | Singularly Speaking | 138 | x | x | x | x | x | x | | | x | | | | |
| | Sportsmania | 140 | | | | | x | | x | | | | | | |
| | Team Huddle | 144 | x | x | | | | x | | | x | | x | | |
| | Trash Collector | 146 | | | | | x | | | | | | | | x |
| Familiarizing | ATZRR | 64 | x | | x | | | x | | | x | | | | |
| | BRAVO! | 66 | x | x | x | x | x | x | | x | | | | x | |
| | Bursting Balloons | 68 | x | | x | | | x | | | x | | x | | |
| | Card Match | 70 | | x | | | | x | | x | | x | | | |
| | Chart Chase | 72 | x | | | | | x | | | x | | | | |
| | Chart Chase 2 | 74 | x | | | | | x | | | | x | | | |
| | Chit Chat | 78 | | x | | | x | x | x | | x | | | | |
| | Find and Fix | 82 | x | x | | | | | | x | | x | | | |
| | Flow Chart Fill-In | 84 | x | x | x | | | x | | x | x | | | | |
| | Frozen Acronyms | 86 | x | | | x | x | x | | | | | | | x |
| | Gallery Guessing | 90 | x | | x | x | | x | x | | | | | | |
| | Group Work | 92 | | x | | | | | x | x | | | x | | |
| | I Object | 96 | | x | | | | | | x | x | | x | | |
| | Identification Shuffle | 98 | x | x | x | | | x | | | x | | | | |
| | Interactive Crossword | 100 | x | x | x | x | x | x | x | | | | | | x |
| | Interactive Word Search | 102 | x | x | x | x | x | x | x | | | | | | x |
| | Literary Assumptions | 104 | x | x | x | x | x | | | | x | | | | |
| | Pop Quiz | 118 | x | x | x | | | x | | | | | | | x |
| | ResponseWare | 128 | x | x | x | x | x | x | | x | | | | x | |
| | Singularly Speaking | 138 | x | x | x | x | x | x | | | x | | | | |
| Innovating New Ideas | BRAVO! | 66 | x | x | x | x | x | x | | x | | | | x | |
| | Chart Chase | 72 | x | | | | | x | | | x | | | | |
| | Chart Chase 2 | 74 | x | | | | | x | | | | x | | | |
| | Chit Chat | 78 | | x | | | x | x | x | | | | | | |
| | Group Work | 92 | | x | | | | | x | x | | | x | | |
| | Heart Smart | 94 | | | | | x | | | | | | | | x |
| | I Object | 96 | | x | | | | | | x | x | | x | | |
| | Pop Ups | 120 | | x | | | x | x | x | | | | | | x |
| | ResponseWare | 128 | x | x | x | x | x | x | | x | | | | x | |
| | Team Huddle | 144 | x | x | | | | x | | | x | | x | | |

| | | Type of Interaction | | | | | | Tools Required | | | | | | |
|---|---|---|---|---|---|---|---|---|---|---|---|---|---|---|
| Name | Page | C | L | O | S | E | R | Group Text Chat | 2-way Audio | Group White-board | White-board | Break Out Rooms | App Share | Poll |
| **Introduce New Concept** | | | | | | | | | | | | | | |
| BRAVO! | 66 | x | x | x | x | x | x | x | | | | | x | |
| Chit Chat | 78 | | x | | | x | x | x | | | | | | |
| Double Trouble | 80 | | | x | x | x | | | | x | | | | |
| Find and Fix | 82 | x | x | | | | | x | | x | | | | |
| Frozen Acronyms | 86 | | x | | | x | x | x | | | | | | x |
| Gallery Guessing | 90 | x | | x | x | | x | x | | | | | | |
| I Object | 96 | | x | | | | | x | | x | | x | | |
| Identification Shuffle | 98 | x | x | x | | | x | | | x | | | | |
| Interactive Crossword | 100 | x | x | x | x | x | x | x | | | | | | x |
| Interactive Word Search | 102 | x | x | x | x | x | x | x | | | | | | x |
| Literary Assumptions | 104 | x | x | x | x | x | | | | x | | | | |
| Mastermind Mix | 108 | | | x | | x | | | x | x | | x | | |
| Pesky Palindromes | 116 | | | x | x | x | | x | | | | | | |
| Pop Quiz | 118 | x | x | x | | | x | | | | | | | x |
| Pop Ups | 120 | | x | | | x | x | x | | | | | | x |
| Q it Up | 122 | x | | x | | x | x | | | | x | | | |
| ResponseWare | 128 | x | x | x | x | x | x | x | | | | | x | |
| Reversible Reflection | 130 | | | x | x | x | | x | | | | | | |
| Riddle Me This | 132 | | | x | x | x | | x | | | | | | |
| Seek and Solve | 134 | x | | x | | | x | | | x | | | | |
| Singularly Speaking | 138 | x | x | x | x | x | x | | | x | | | | |
| Team Huddle | 144 | x | x | | | | x | | | x | | x | | |
| WEBB"O" | 150 | x | | x | | x | x | x | | | x | | | |
| **Previewing Material** | | | | | | | | | | | | | | |
| BRAVO! | 66 | x | x | x | x | x | x | x | | | | | x | |
| Bursting Balloons | 68 | x | | x | | | | | | x | | x | | |
| Card Match | 70 | | x | | | | | | x | | x | | | |
| Flow Chart Fill-In | 84 | x | x | x | | | | x | | x | | | | |
| Fulfilling Fill-in the Blanks | 88 | | x | x | | x | x | | | | x | | | |
| I Object | 96 | | x | | | | | x | | x | | x | | |
| Identification Shuffle | 98 | x | x | x | | | x | | | x | | | | |
| Interactive Crossword | 100 | x | x | x | x | x | x | x | | | | | | x |
| Interactive Word Search | 102 | x | x | x | x | x | x | x | | | | | | x |
| Pop Quiz | 118 | x | x | x | | | x | | | | | | | x |
| Pop Ups | 120 | | x | | | x | x | x | | | | | | x |
| ResponseWare | 128 | x | x | x | x | x | x | x | | | | | x | |
| Seek and Solve | 134 | x | | x | | | x | | | x | | | | |
| Team Huddle | 144 | x | x | | | | x | | | x | | x | | |
| WEBB"O" | 150 | x | | x | | x | x | x | | | x | | | |
| **Recall Background Knowledge** | | | | | | | | | | | | | | |
| ATZRR | 64 | x | | x | | | x | | | x | | | | |
| BRAVO! | 66 | x | x | x | x | x | x | x | | | | | x | |
| Bursting Balloons | 68 | x | | x | | | x | | | x | | x | | |
| Card Match | 70 | | x | | | | x | | x | | x | | | |
| Chart Chase | 72 | x | | | | | x | | | x | | | | |
| Chart Chase 2 | 74 | x | | | | | x | | | | x | | | |
| Chit Chat | 78 | | x | | | x | x | x | | | | | | |
| Find and Fix | 82 | x | x | | | | x | | | x | | | | |
| Flow Chart Fill-In | 84 | x | x | x | | | x | x | | x | | | | |
| Frozen Acronyms | 86 | | x | | | x | x | x | | | | | | x |
| Gallery Guessing | 90 | x | | x | x | | x | x | | | | | | |
| Group Work | 92 | | x | | | | x | | x | | | x | | |
| Heart Smart | 94 | | | | x | | | | | | | | | x |
| Identification Shuffle | 98 | x | x | x | | | x | | | x | | | | |
| Interactive Crossword | 100 | x | x | x | x | x | x | x | | | | | | x |
| Literary Assumptions | 104 | x | x | x | x | x | | | | x | | | | |
| Pop Quiz | 118 | x | x | x | | | x | | | | | | | x |
| ResponseWare | 128 | x | x | x | x | x | x | | x | | | | x | |
| Singularly Speaking | 138 | x | x | x | x | x | x | | | x | | | | |
| Under, Over, Around... | 148 | | | | | x | x | x | | x | | | | |

| | Name of Activity | Page | C | L | O | S | E | R | Group Text Chat | 2-way Audio | Group White-board | White-board | Break Out Rooms | App Share | Poll |
|---|---|---|---|---|---|---|---|---|---|---|---|---|---|---|---|
| **Recall Information-Existing Schemas** | ATZRR | 64 | x | | x | | | x | | | x | | | | |
| | BRAVO! | 66 | x | x | x | x | x | x | | x | | | | x | |
| | Bursting Balloons | 68 | x | | x | | | x | | | x | | x | | |
| | Card Match | 70 | | x | | | | x | | | x | x | | | |
| | Find and Fix | 82 | x | x | | | | | x | | x | | | | |
| | Flow Chart Fill-In | 84 | x | x | x | | | x | | | x | x | | | |
| | Frozen Acronyms | 86 | | x | | | x | x | | | | | | | x |
| | Gallery Guessing | 90 | x | | x | x | | x | x | | | | | | |
| | Group Work | 92 | | x | | | | | | x | x | | x | | |
| | Heart Smart | 94 | | | | x | | | | | | | | | x |
| | I Object | 96 | | x | | | | | | x | x | | x | | |
| | Identification Shuffle | 98 | x | x | x | | | x | | | x | | | | |
| | Literary Assumptions | 104 | x | x | x | x | x | | | | x | | | | |
| | Pop Quiz | 118 | x | x | x | | | x | | | | | | | x |
| | Pop Ups | 120 | | x | | | x | x | | | | | | | x |
| | ResponseWare | 128 | x | x | x | x | x | x | | x | | | | x | |
| | Seek and Solve | 134 | x | | x | | | x | | | x | | | | |
| | Singularly Speaking | 138 | x | x | x | x | x | x | | | x | | | | |
| | Under, Over, Around… | 148 | | | | | x | x | x | | x | | | | |
| **Refocus Learner** | ATZRR | 64 | x | | x | | | x | | | x | | | | |
| | BRAVO! | 66 | x | x | x | x | x | x | | x | | | | x | |
| | Bursting Balloons | 68 | x | | x | | | x | | | x | | x | | |
| | Chart Chase | 72 | x | | | | | x | | | x | | | | |
| | Chart Chase 2 | 74 | x | | | | | x | | | | x | | | |
| | Chit Chat | 78 | | x | | | x | x | x | | | | | | |
| | Double Trouble | 80 | | | x | x | x | | | | x | | | | |
| | Flow Chart Fill-In | 84 | x | x | | | | x | | | x | x | | | |
| | Fulfilling Fill-in the Blanks | 88 | | x | x | | x | x | | | | x | | | |
| | Gallery Guessing | 90 | x | | x | x | | x | x | | | | | | |
| | Heart Smart | 94 | | | | x | | | | | | | | | x |
| | I Object | 96 | | x | | | | | | x | x | | x | | |
| | Interactive Crossword | 100 | x | x | x | x | x | x | x | | | | | | x |
| | Interactive Word Search | 102 | x | x | x | x | x | | x | x | | | | | x |
| | Literary Assumptions | 104 | x | x | x | x | x | | | | x | | | | |
| | One and Done Break | 110 | | | | | | x | | | | x | | | |
| | Pesky Palindromes | 116 | | | x | x | x | | x | | | | | | |
| | Pop Quiz | 118 | x | x | x | | | x | | | | | | | x |
| | ResponseWare | 128 | x | x | x | x | x | x | | x | | | | x | |
| | Reversible Reflection | 130 | | | x | x | x | | x | | | | | | |
| | Singularly Speaking | 138 | x | x | x | x | x | | | | x | | | | |
| | Under, Over, Around… | 148 | | | | | x | x | x | | x | | | | |
| | Who Done It? | 152 | x | | | | x | x | x | | | | | | |
| **Review** | ATZRR | 64 | x | | x | | | x | | | x | | | | |
| | BRAVO! | 66 | x | x | x | x | x | x | | x | | | | x | |
| | Bursting Balloons | 68 | x | | x | | | x | | | x | | x | | |
| | Card Match | 70 | | x | | | | x | | | x | x | | | |
| | Chart Chase | 72 | x | | | | | x | | | x | | | | |
| | Chart Chase 2 | 74 | x | | | | | x | | | | x | | | |
| | Check and Balance | 76 | x | x | | | | | | x | x | | | | |
| | Chit Chat | 78 | | x | | | x | x | x | | | | | | |
| | Flow Chart Fill-In | 84 | x | x | x | | | x | | x | x | | | | |
| | Frozen Acronyms | 86 | | x | | | x | x | | | | | | | x |
| | Gallery Guessing | 90 | x | | x | x | | x | x | | | | | | |
| | Group Work | 92 | | x | | | | | | x | x | | x | | |
| | Heart Smart | 94 | | | | x | | | | | | | | | x |
| | I Object | 96 | | x | | | | | | x | x | | x | | |
| | Identification Shuffle | 98 | x | x | x | | | x | | | x | | | | |
| | Pop Quiz | 118 | x | x | x | | | x | | | | | | | x |
| | ResponseWare | 128 | x | x | x | x | x | | x | x | | | | x | |
| | Under, Over, Around… | 148 | | | | | x | x | x | | x | | | | |
| | Who Done It? | 152 | x | | | | x | x | x | | | | | | |
| **Teach New Material** | BRAVO! | 66 | x | x | x | x | x | x | | x | | | | x | |
| | Flow Chart Fill-In | 84 | x | x | x | | | x | | x | x | | | | |
| | Frozen Acronyms | 86 | | x | | | x | x | | | | | | | x |
| | Group Work | 92 | | x | | | | | | x | x | | x | | |
| | Heart Smart | 94 | | | | x | | | | | | | | | x |
| | I Object | 96 | | x | | | | | | x | x | | x | | |
| | Identification Shuffle | 98 | x | x | x | | | R | | | x | | | | |
| | Literary Assumptions | 104 | x | x | x | x | x | | | | x | | | | |
| | Pop Quiz | 118 | x | x | x | | | x | | | | | | | x |
| | Pop Ups | 120 | | x | | | x | x | | | | | | | x |
| | ResponseWare | 128 | x | x | x | x | x | x | | x | | | | x | |
| | Singularly Speaking | 138 | x | x | x | x | x | | | | x | | | | |
| | Team Huddle | 144 | x | x | | | | x | | | x | | x | | |

# ABOUT THE AUTHOR

Over the past five years, Becky Pike Pluth, M.Ed., has designed and delivered more than 100 interactive webinars on a variety of topics, including sales, customer service, product training and compliance. Her in-person sessions at the Training 2009 and 2010 conferences drew standing-room-only audiences. With more than 13 years of experience in training delivery and design, project management and business operations, she has worked with 16 of the Fortune 100 companies.

In designing these interactive webinar tools, Pluth has utilized sustainable change and adult learning principles. Her methods are transferable, immediately applicable and highly effective. A trained educator, Pluth expanded into corporate training after completing her master's degree in teaching and learning.

Pluth is vice president of training and development at The Bob Pike Group, which consults on participant-centered training. She is also the author of *101 Movie Clips that Teach and Train*.

## 101 MOVIE CLIPS THAT TEACH & TRAIN

Using short clips from movies can relay learning points more dramatically and quickly than any lecture. Let *101 Movie Clips that Teach & Train* jumpstart your creativity for lesson planning or training design by providing you with the perfect movie clip for more than 100 topics, including discrimination, leadership, team building and sales. Each clip comes with cueing times, plot summary, scene context and cogent discussion questions. All topics are cross-referenced so you can easily find the perfect clip for your teaching or training needs.

To purchase this title, go to 101MovieClips.com or call 1-612-875-3634.

## WEBINARS WITH WOW FACTOR READY-TO-GO SLIDES

Quick-start your next interactive webinar with well-designed PowerPoint slides! The slides that accompany the interactivities in chapter 6 are available for you to use in your next online training. Save yourself a lot of time searching for just the right images and frustration in designing the slides. There are 60 slides in all to give your session WoW!

To purchase the slide decks, go to WebinarsWithWowFactor.com.